DEPRESSION
AND WHAT TO DO ABOUT IT

(THE DEPRESSED CHRISTIAN - REVISED)

Some Facts and Opinions about Depression

By Rev. Gerald F. Mundfrom

First Printing 1983
Entitled: "The Depressed Christian"

Copy right 1994 - Rev. Gerald F. Mundfrom
Library of Congress Card Number: 94-78061
ISBN: 0-9615494-4-0

Published by:
Mercy and Truth Publishers
312 235th Street
Osceola, Wisconsin 54020-5943

Printed by:
Sunshine Graphics
1023 East Highway 95
Cambridge, Minnesota 55008

DEDICATION

I dedicate this book--to my six children: John, Daniel, Ruth, Rachel, Priscilla and Stephen; who from a very young age have sought to live 'godly lives and have greatly gladdened the hearts of their mother and father;
--and to my three daughters-in-law: Lorilee, Elaine and Joanne; and my three sons-in-law: Mark, Martin and Bill who have added so much to our family.

TABLE OF CONTENT

Title page----------------------------------i
Dedication----------------------------------ii
Table of Contents---------------------------iii
Glossary------------------------------------v
Preface-------------------------------------vi

I. DEPRESSION AS IT RELATES TO THE SOUL
   1. Discouragement and Encouragement-----1
   2. What is Depression-------------------5
   3. Reasons Why God Wills Depression-----15
   4. Sin and Depression-------------------22
   5. God Purges His Own-------------------29

II. DEPRESSION AS IT RELATES TO OUR BODY
   6. How Our Physical and Mental
      Systems Compare--------------------34
   7. Self Pity and Living in Regret-------41
   8. Confusion---------------------------45
   9. The Weary Christian Warrior----------54

III. WHAT TO DO WHEN DEPRESSED
   10. Waiting on the Lord-----------------59
   11. Depression as a Temptation----------69
   12. Being Encouraged--------------------75
   13. Encouragement Found in God's Word---89
   14. Being Idle--------------------------93
   15. Daydreaming-------------------------97
   16. Work--------------------------------100
   17. Procrastination---------------------103
   18. Too Much Ambition-------------------107
   19. Fear--------------------------------108
   20. Worry-------------------------------114
   21. Prayer and Bible Study--------------118
   22. Grief-------------------------------129
   23. Growing in Grace and Holiness-------132

IV. SOME CAUSES OF CERTAIN ABNORMAL
    DISORDERS
   24. The Hypochondriac-------------------134
   25. Neurotic Pain-----------------------138
   26. Stress as it Relates to Certain
      Physical Disorders-----------------140
   27. Paranoid or Bitter Feelings Toward
      Others-----------------------------141
   28. Illusions of Grandeur---------------146
   29. Alcoholism--------------------------148

    30. Drugs and Shock Treatments---------154
V. MINISTERING TO THE DEPRESSED
    31. How to Minister to the
           Depressed--------------------------156
    32. A Word to the Pastors--------------169
    33. Uncovering the Subconscious--------172
VI. GOD USES SUFFERING FOR GOOD
    34. How Christian Joy and Suffering
           Relate-----------------------------176
    35. The Cost of Following Jesus--------184
VII. MEN AND WOMEN WHOM GOD TESTED
    36. Some Whom God Tested---------------194
    37. Job, Jeremiah, and Elijah----------197
VIII. APPENDIX
    38. Some Stresses that May Contribute
           to Depression----------------------210
    39. Symptoms of Acute or Clinical
           Depression-------------------------213
    40. How to Maintain or Regain Your
           Mental Health---------------------215
    41. Some Suggestions for Helping a
           Depressed Loved One------------219

GLOSSARY

Note: Words may have different meanings to different people. In order to avoid misunderstanding, this glossary expresses the meaning of the term as understood by the author and as used in this book.

(1) Abnormal Disorder - a behavior pattern which is drastically different from the accepted norm of society.

(2) Acute or Clinical Depression - Deep feelings of sadness, uncontrollable by the patient, which may interfere with his ability to concentrate and function normally.

(3) Alcoholic - A person who has lost his willpower to abstain from (or limit) his drinking of alcoholic beverages.

(4) Depression - any feeling or feelings of sadness which overtake a person. It can affect some people to a greater degree than others.

(5) Hypochondriac - a patient who seems to welcome the symptoms of physical illness, where there is no evidence of such illness, because they meet some need, such as receiving recognition, in his life.

(6) Illusions of Grandeur - a temporary feeling of extreme lightheartedness and optimism in a person suffering from acute depression.

(7) Neurotic - A patient who has symptoms of a physical illness brought about by extreme worry or stress.

(8) Paranoia - a mental disorder causing the patient to mistrust and sometimes hate people without a cause.

(9) Subconscious - a memory bank from which thoughts can be released and brought into the conscious memory by key reminders or suggestions.

PREFACE

We have today a great epidemic of depression--so much so that it has become a major concern to our society. Many Christians are suffering from depression or extreme unhappiness. This state is very confusing to them, especially in light of the fact that today's preaching puts a great deal of stress on joy and happiness. This, they say, is the reward of being a Christian. There are those who claim to have the secret of obtaining such bliss, and are very eager to reveal their secret to others.

However, it seems that the more stress there is on happiness, the greater is the epidemic, especially among Christians. We are often quick to conclude that there must be something wrong, something displeasing to God, in these depressed Christians' faith, since their lot seems to be depression instead of joy and happiness. Some even go so far as to conclude that they must be under the power of the devil in some way, or that they may be demon-possessed.

But could it be that there is something wrong with our preaching, with the way we talk about Christianity as the way of joy and happiness? I truly believe there is! We are forgetting the cross of the Christian. Jesus did not promise an easy way for His own on earth, should they choose to follow Him. Oh, there would be joy, especially in heaven, but there would also be sorrow and trials. Jesus said to those who wanted to follow Him, "Whosoever will come after me, let him deny himself, and take up his cross, and follow me" (Mark 8:34).

God looks upon suffering, including depression, differently from man. He at times wills it for His own, not because they have grievously sinned, but in order to prepare them for greater use (John 15:2b).

This book is primarily written for the encouragement of the discouraged, depressed Christian to help him understand his situation, to assure him that his feelings of unhappiness and suffering are not unusual, and that such suffering is not in vain, that he is not a less mature Christian because of his suffering, that God has not forsaken him but has a purpose in his suffering and in His good time will work it all out for good (Rom. 8:28).

In writing this book I draw heavily from my own experience with depression (having spent some time as a patient in a mental hospital), from the experience of others whom I have counseled, and upon Biblical truth.

My approach to this subject may be somewhat different from the ordinary. I have also taken the freedom to state my opinion on certain matters that have not been definitely proven scientifically. I realize that what I write is far from all-inclusive.

However, because of my experience and training, and because I have been a help to others with a similar experience, I wish to share the insights which I have gained in a language understandable to the laity.

I am reminded of the apostle Paul (II Cor. 1:4-8) who spoke of comforting those who were suffering with the comfort (godly comfort) with which he was comforted. Paul's suffering enabled him to do this. The Scripture also states that because Jesus suffered (Hebr. 4:15), He can be touched so as to sympathize with us in our suffering (infirmities).

This is my aim in my writing. Even as I found comfort and hope in the midst of suffering, I hope to bring hope and comfort to others who are suffering by sharing what I learned from my experience. (I also refer you to my book, MY EXPERIENCE WITH CLINICAL DEPRESSION, which tells of my suffering in detail.)

As source material I draw heavily from the King James Version of the Bible.

In view of what I have said above, I submit the following qualifications which enable me to write this book.

One, I am a Christian from early childhood.

Two, I am a Lutheran pastor and have a formal education in the study of Scripture.

Three, I have had thirty years' experience serving as a parish pastor.

Four, I have had some clinical training and done reading on the subject of depression and mental illness.

Five, I have previously done some speaking and writing on this subject.

Six, God saw fit to lead me through a period of mental illness with great depression. I spent several months in a mental hospital, which was like a schooling, enabling me to empathize with the depressed and heavy-hearted Christian in his testings.

Seven, my counseling and writing has proven helpful to the depressed.

Eight, during the Second World War I was in the medical branch of the army and have had experience in helping the sick and suffering.

In writing the first edition of this book I am indebted and appreciative to the following: my brother-in-law, the Rev. Wilfred Lindquist; my wife, Margaret; and my two daughters, Rachel and Priscilla for help in editing and typing; and to my sister-in-law, Dr. Mary Lindquist, who read the manuscript and made suggestions.

In rewriting this second edition I greatly appreciate the suggestions given by Jerry Hjelden and the editing done by the Rev. Edward A. Johnson.

I am also indebted and appreciative to many friends and acquaintances over the years who have encouraged me in this type of ministry; and most of all to God who has called, burdened and led me in this particular way.

My heart and prayerful desire is that the thoughts here shared might, directly or indirectly, be a help and an encouragement to some Christians who are undergoing great testings.

Rev. Gerald F. Mundfrom

I. DEPRESSION AS IT RELATES TO THE SOUL

1. Discouragement and Encouragement

There are many problems, storms, stresses, anxieties, and much sickness and suffering in this world. These things may cause a person to become tired, weary, discouraged, depressed or defeated. Individuals face these problems and suffer the effects in varying degrees.

Some who live in gross, open sin (at least for a season) bring many of these problems upon themselves. They usually enjoy the sins they are engaged in for a season and find them tempting and exciting. But sooner or later the ill effects of sin catch up with them and cloud their joy, often driving them to despair.

A Biblical example of this type of person is King David, who at one time in his life yielded to temptation and became guilty of adultery and murder. In Psalm 51 David expressed his great anguish of soul as he begs God for mercy. "...and my sin is ever before me" (vs. 3b).

But there is also the prosperous, physically healthy individual who does not seem to be greatly troubled in any way nor have a problem with weariness, discouragement or depression. He is not a Christian, although he may go to church and think himself a Christian. He believes in honesty and is at peace with almost everyone. He very likely has many friends. He is greatly enjoying life here on earth. He has gathered certain comforts and luxuries around himself, and his one ambition is to excel more and more in these earthly possessions, pleasures and comforts. He wishes he could remain here on earth forever and lives as though he will. His treasures are all on earth, with none in heaven, and this is where his heart is. He is quite satisfied with life as he finds it.

An outstanding example of this person is the greedy farmer in Luke 12:16-20, who was only interested in enjoying the earthly riches which he had been able to gather for himself. However, it is not only the farmer who can be overly dedicated to the things of this world to the neglect of his soul's need. There are many in all walks of life who are busy building a little kingdom for themselves on this earth which they hope to enjoy for a long, long time. The building of this kingdom takes up all their time and is their greatest interest. It is their first love.

But what about the dedicated Christian who is engaged with Jesus in a warfare against sin and evil, a warfare which, like any other warfare, has its worries, stresses, discomforts, threats, dangers and suffering, and which also often brings ridicule, persecution and sometimes martyrdom?

This dedicated Christian loves Jesus and all He stands for. He hates sin and evil. He is burdened for the lost and finds this to be a heavy burden to carry. He has taken up his cross (Mk. 8:34) as a soldier takes up his arms. He is ready to pay the price, whatever needed, to enter and hold his place in that warfare. He does not find life on earth all that pleasant and is looking forward to being in heaven with Jesus forever. This Christian feels the heat of the battle and all the stresses that accompany the warfare. He may suffer its effects and become tired, weary, discouraged or depressed. We have examples in the Bible such as Job, Joseph, David, Elijah, Nehemiah, Jeremiah, Paul and others.

Jesus said in Mark 8:34-36: "Whosoever will come after me, let him deny himself, and take up his cross, and follow me. For whosoever will save his life (those who live only for themselves and this world shall lose it; but whosoever shall lose his life for my sake and the gospel's, the same shall save it. For what shall it profit a man if he shall gain the whole world and lose his own soul?"

Jesus is looking for dedicated soldiers of the cross who will dare risk everything they have (if need be), and who are willing to face the war against sin and evil with Him.

However, though Jesus wills to lead us into the Christian warfare in order that His kingdom on earth might advance, He promises to sustain us and uphold us in that warfare. He has said, "Lo, I am with you alway, even unto the end of the world" (Mt. 28:20b). Paul, who was a great Christian warrior, testifies to his faith in Jesus' promises when he quotes Jesus as saying, "My grace is sufficient" (II Cor. 12:9). Because of this promise Paul dared to face the Christian warfare.

The fight is not easy. The enemy is real and powerful. Often it may seem that Satan is winning more battles than God is. After many centuries of time, evil seems more rampant than ever.

Many would tell us that we should never become discouraged or depressed as a Christian, as if to do so would be a sin. But we can't always help it when this happens to us. No one wants to become discouraged. It is not something we crave as we might crave a sinful habit. But it comes upon us like a storm. Often circumstances in life will bring it on, and unless we have no feelings, we are going to become discouraged. At such times we might be able to hide our discouragement from others, but deep down within we feel sad and disheartened.

But then, as we become weary and low, we can go to Jesus and find a rest and comfort in Him. "Come unto Me," Jesus says, "all ye that labor and are heavy laden (the Christian warrior) and I will give you rest" (Mt. 11:28). Here we see no rebuke on the part of Jesus to the Christian for being weary and sad, even discouraged, as if it were a sin. Rather, we sense that Jesus expects us to become tired and weary when we labor and fight the Christian warfare for His name's sake.

The military does not tell its fighting men that they should not get tired, weary or discouraged, but expects them to give of themselves so that they do become tired and weary, risking danger and life all for the cause of the war. But then the military offers food and rest for the tired and weary, and medical care for the wounded; and they honor their dead.

In the same way the Christian soldier is expected to spend himself in the Christian warfare, all for the cause of Christ. And as he becomes weary and discouraged, he is invited to come again and again to Jesus for restoration.

It is not a sin to become weary and discouraged in the Christian warfare, but we are not to give up. Nor need we give up, because God's grace is available and is ours for the asking.

2. What is Depression?

It has become difficult to define depression because some read more and some less into the meaning.

To some it has a broad meaning relating to a number of causes. To others it has a specific meaning relating to only a limited number of causes. Other terms, such as "burnout" are used to describe the illness.

There seems to be a tendency to avoid calling it depression. In writing this book, however, I have preferred using a broad definition in explaining the meaning of depression.

Clinical or acute depression has a feeling all its own. It is a most miserable, sad feeling unlike anything else which the human body might suffer. To describe what it feels like, to someone who has never experienced it, is as difficult as it would be to explain what daylight is like to a man born blind.

But the person who has experienced this major type of depression needs no definition. He well knows what it is like from experience. And he can relate his experience to anyone who has had a similar experience.

In writing this book I think of depression as including any and all feelings of sadness, such as feelings of guilt, failure, defeat, grief, loneliness, fatigue, fear, confusion, boredom, listlessness, lack of self-esteem, restlessness, helplessness, doubt about God, and doubt about his or her salvation. He may experience several of these most miserable feelings at the same time.

When a person becomes depressed, he becomes a somewhat different person from what he was before. Others, even those who were very close, such as relatives and close friends, notice this. They find it hard to communicate with this seemingly different person who has lost interest in what formerly interested him. Because the deeply depressed person has become somewhat withdrawn, they find it hard to fellowship with him. They now seem to have little in common. They feel uneasy in his presence, as though they were with some stranger whom they hardly know. They don't understand what has happened to this person. Not knowing how to communicate with this seeming stranger they may avoid him.

In turn, the depressed person does not understand the reason for the change in attitude on the part of former friends and relatives, and he feels even more depressed.

Little problems become major problems. He often loses interest in what is going on around him, in things he formerly was interested in or involved in and considered to be important. He may feel unwanted, in the way, useless, or not loved, and that he is a problem to everyone--especially close-by loved ones. He may feel that it would be better for himself and all concerned if he were out of the way, and he may be tempted to commit suicide.

In a normal person any one or more of the above miserable feelings may be realized from time to time in a lesser degree. Circumstances in life often cause such unhappy feelings. However, a normal person can usually find a way to cope with such feelings, and they soon go away. He may get involved in a work project, go on a short trip, go see a friend, or do something else from what is routine in order to take his mind off his worries and that which is depressing to him. If he is a Christian, he will find encouragement and help in prayer and from God's Word. He learns to wait on God for the help and encouragement he needs.

In acute depression, which I suffered in 1964, and which often puts a patient in the hospital, the depressed feeling is much more intense and clings to the patient like glue, refusing to leave--no matter to what extent the patient tries to get involved in an attempt to divert his mind to something else besides that which is depressing to him.

In acute depression the deep, sad, agonizing feelings enslave the person to such an extent that he cannot release himself from them for even a moment. They haunt him day and night and greatly interfere with his ability to sleep--especially at night. The patient feels so helpless in the grip of his depressed, sad feelings that he begins to think there is no escape or hope of ever becoming released from them, or in ever having any peace and joy in life again.

His worries are forever in the center of his thinking and seem to block any other thoughts from entering into his conscious mind. He finds it to be very difficult and even impossible to give his full attention to anything else besides his worries, or to get involved in any activity which involves concentration.

In his attempt to think something through, or reason something out for himself, his thinking just seems automatically to shift to his worries and all kinds of unpleasant thoughts. He is easily distracted from anything which challenges his concentration. His memory is affected especially in the remembering of names and places. Because his ability to concentrate is affected, he is unable to work or do many things he once was able to do.

He finds it very difficult to make

decisions, especially major decisions. He dreads the thought of having to do so and tends to put it off as long as he can. He would prefer having others decide for him. He is unable to separate the advantages from the disadvantages and logically think a matter through. Small decisions become major decisions. He may spend much time deciding on such a trivial matter as what color of socks to wear, which way to go in taking a walk, or which shoes to buy. He worries about the outcome should he make the wrong decision, or about what people might think of him.

He feels that he does not know the issues involved in making a wise decision. He lacks the courage to take a chance which all decision-making involves to some degree. With the normal person, thinking through and deciding on something can be compared to facing a stop light which is telling him to wait while he thinks the matter through. Then, if he should come to the conclusion that it would be advantageous to go ahead and decide favorably on the matter being considered, the red stop light changes to green for go, and he gains the freedom to go ahead. With a deeply depressed person the red stop light never changes to green. He continues to remain in a indecisive frame of mind.

The person suffering from acute depression feels hemmed in or pressed down with a multitude of problems which he cannot solve. He feels tired, worn out, as if he would like to go to bed and sleep for a very long time, but when in bed he cannot sleep.

When I was suffering from acute depression, I felt as if I could not breathe deeply. I could not breathe a sigh of relief which I longed to do. It seemed to me that if I could only do this, I would feel much better. I had the feeling that something very heavy was pressing on my chest preventing me from taking a very deep breath of air. If only I could breathe deeply enough so as to get under this terrible, depressed feeling, and if I then exhaled, I should be able to expel the depression. So it seemed. But the depression was rooted so deep within me that I could not breathe deeply enough to exhale it.

However, even though a deeply depressed person may have all or some of the above miserable feelings, that does not necessarily mean that the situation is as he feels it to be. For example, he may feel that he is a failure, when he is not a failure at all. He may feel that he is no longer a Christian, being plagued with many doubts yet having done nothing to break his relationship with Christ.

Depression can be experienced by degrees. Some people are more depressed than others. One may be more depressed at one time than at another time. Acute or clinical depression can also be felt to a greater or lesser degree at different times. However, at the same time there is a constant depressed feeling which will not leave or let go day or night. Many acutely depressed people feel the worst in the morning or just before getting out of bed. (It has been said that most suicides occur in the morning due to poorer blood circulation at that time of the day.)

The clinically depressed person often finds it difficult to communicate with other people because of his inability to concentrate. He may start to say something, then suffer a memory block and not be able to finish his sentence.

He is often overcome with an acute sense of fear. He feels helpless in the midst of many circumstances and can do nothing about this feeling. Things he once could do he now cannot. He wonders how he will ever be able to face the future. The future is a threat to him.

He wonders if anyone has ever suffered as he is suffering. So miserable is his feeling that he finds it hard and even impossible to describe. This makes him feel very alone. He wonders if anyone can possibly understand what he is going through.

There seems to be a need for the depressed person to relate his feelings to someone. He feels that if there is to be any hope of a cure, he must describe his symptoms to someone. He longs to confide in someone and tell that someone how he feels. Yet his limited concentration makes it impossible to describe the complicated, miserable feeling which he is experiencing.

Then he feels even more depressed. He asks himself, "If I cannot even describe the symptoms, how can anyone prescribe a cure?" He feels that there must not be any hope for a cure, and this frightens him.

If you have experienced some acute depression and can put yourself in the depressed person's place and help him to express his miserable feeling, he will be grateful to you and will be helped to realize that someone understands and knows what he is going through; that he is not alone and not the only one who has experienced this kind of suffering.

A deeply depressed person may find it difficult to pray as he once was able to do. In his attempt to pray, as in his attempt to communicate, he suffers mental blocks and his mind goes wandering off in another direction. He feels that he is not getting through to God, to Jesus, and he wonders if He really understands what he is going through.

He may find it very difficult and even impossible to read his Bible (or anything else) so that it makes sense to him. He is able to pronounce the words with his mind, but he cannot obtain the thought.

When I was suffering from acute depression I would read the same paragraph over and over again in my Bible. But afterwards I still did not know what the paragraph was all about.

The depressed person's lack of ability to pray and read the Bible greatly adds to his guilt feeling. He hears reports from others of how they were helped and comforted through prayer and the reading of God's Word, but now, in his attempt to receive help and encouragement in the same way, he finds this avenue seemingly closed to him. This only adds to his feeling of loneliness and of seemingly being deserted by God. He wonders if he has sunk so low in his depressed state that even God cannot or will not help him. It all adds to his feeling of utter hopelessness.

The depressed person finds little or nothing for which he can rejoice or be thankful. His depressed feelings overshadow everything he once enjoyed. He is like a car with a faulty carburetor. The spark plugs and tires may be new, but because the carburetor does not work, neither are these other parts able to function. So with depression. It takes all the joy out of life. Even the good things in life seem to turn sour.

No matter what he looks at, or whom he talks to, he feels a sense of envy (at least I did). Everyone else seems to have something to live for in which they seem to find at least a measure of joy or satisfaction. But to the deeply depressed there are only clouds without sunshine. Life has lost all meaning. And because of his miserable feelings along with his inability to pray and read the Bible, he doubts his standing with God and doesn't know what to do about his problem. God seems so distant! His faith is weak! He may have felt sure about a place in heaven after death at one time, but now he has no such assurance and wonders if heaven might not have slipped away from him, never to be regained. He feels deserted by God. He wonders if he is still a Christian even though previously he has surrendered his life to Jesus and has remained faithful. It is not because of what he has done or failed to do that he doubts his salvation, but because of all the miserable feelings he is experiencing.

The deeply depressed person tends to withdraw from people. He feels ill at ease in their presence. Even close friends and relatives seem distant. His inability to concentrate and communicate tend to put them in a different world.

The deeply depressed person cannot daydream as he once was able to do. In every such dream, he runs up against his present limitations and cannot imagine that it will ever again be as it once was. The way back to the mental health he once enjoyed seems hopeless and impossible. When others tell him he will get better, he wonders how, and feels that their encouragement is either only wishful thinking on their part or that they do not really know the seriousness of his condition--or if they know, they are trying to spare him the awful truth of his condition by withholding it from him.

The acutely depressed person often does not know why he is depressed and so extremely unhappy. "Why do I have this awful miserable, sad feeling all of the time?" Like the Psalmist (Psalm 43:5) he

- 12 -

asks the question, "Why art thou cast down, O my soul? And why art thou disquieted within me?" Also, like this psalmist, he may be aware of the goodness of God (in spite of his doubts) but still is extremely unhappy, but does not know why, or what to do about it.

Others may remind him of the many things he should be thankful for and which should lift his spirits. He may agree and try to let these things crowd out the despondency, but the depression remains as acute as ever. Something seems to be blocking the spirit of thanksgiving, joy and happiness from coming in and filling his heart, and he does not know what it is. He feels helpless and enslaved.

This unknown cause is sometimes buried deep in the subconscious mind. Even so it can greatly affect his feelings and cause him to be depressed. If the cause can be surfaced and brought into the conscious mind, the healing from depression is much quicker and will enable the patient to see whether there is anything he can do to remedy the situation.

If the acutely depressed person does know the reason for his depresion, or has some idea what is causing it, he still may not be able to rid himself of the depressed feeling until something is done to alleviate the cause.

In my experience with clinical depression I was not able to figure out the cause for some time. When I realized the cause, I was able to adjust my life accordingly and to cope with the cause and healing came much quicker. I saw those things that were troubling me in a different perspective.

The acutely depressed person feels so miserable that he would like to go to sleep and not wake up for a long, long time, perhaps never. It seems senseless that sleep is the only thing that gives any satisfaction to living. He reasons that he might as well be dead, and prays that he might die. Some are tempted to commit suicide, and some do.

I, too, wanted to die, but God spared me from any temptation to take my own life or cause myself physical harm. Sleep was the only thing that gave me any release from my despondency. However, sleep did not come easily, especially at night.

3. Reasons Why God Wills Depression

It is believed by some that depression is evil and displeasing to God. Some claim that all depression is of the devil, and that it is a sign that God is displeased with that person. Those who counseled Job reasoned this way (Book of Job).

In the life of a Christian, God will use depression for good as He has promised in Rom. 8:28: "And we know that all things work together for good to them who are called according to his purpose." "All things" also includes feelings of depression.

The following reasons may explain why God would want some of His children to go through a period of depression some time during their life time on earth. There could very well be more reasons.

1. God uses depression to teach us many things. To the Christian it is a schooling. God taught me many things as he led me through a time of depression. I sincerely believe it was His will for me to have this experience.

When we come into this world there are many things we need to learn. We learn some things the hard way so that we do not forget them. If I had known, at the time I became depressed, what I now know about how to cope with various types of stress (which caused my depression) I very likely would not have become depressed.

But in our learning we need to start somewhere. I learned much from being depressed which has been helpful in facing problems and in helping others, and for which I thank God. He did work it all out for good.

2. God uses depression to test us. In school we are given tests to see what

we have accomplished in our studies. The further we progress in school, the harder the tests. God also gives tests. He tests His own as John 15:2b plainly tells us: "And every branch that beareth fruit, he purgeth it, that it may bring forth more fruit." It is as we mature as Christians and mature in life that the testings become more trying.

God will test our sincerity. He will test us to see if we will stand on our Christian convictions--to see if we will compromise when under pressure.

He will test our faith in Him and in His Word. He will test our love. And these tests can be depressing.

Our comfort can be that He will help us and be with us in these testings as we look to Him for help. When we take a test in school we cannot expect help from the teacher, who will help us and answer our questions any time prior to the test, but not while taking the test. God is different! He is ready and willing to help us in all of our testings--before, during and after the testing. In fact, a part of the testing is to see to what extent we are ready and willing to wait on God for the answers and help that we need. His grace is all-sufficient (II Cor. 12:9). As we experience God's grace or willingness to help us when tested, our faith in Him is strengthened and becomes established.

3. Sometimes God uses depression to lead us. He may have a new and more challenging route in life for us to travel than we have traveled before. He may draw our attention to this new way by causing us to be depressed with our present situation and to long for a change. Or He may cause us to be depressed in order to prevent us from going a certain way which we have our

hearts set on but which is not according to His will. Or we may become depressed as we anticipate, with some degree of fear, the change we are about to make. God has led me in this way more than once in life. "There is a way which seemeth right unto a man, but the end thereof are the ways of death" (Prov. 14:12).

4. God burdens His own to be concerned or burdened for the lost. This can be very depressing, especially if those lost are loved ones who refuse to have anything to do with Jesus and His Word and despise our witness or our ministering to them.

Such a burden is heavy and painful to carry. We dread the thought of our loved ones spending eternity in hell. But it is God's will for us that we carry such burdens. And God often uses a burdened soul to win a lost soul unto Himself. The ungodly do not face this type of anguish or concern.

I think of the Christian mother or father who longs to see the wayward children come to Jesus. What is it that finally wins these children for the Lord? It is not the smiling faces of these parents but the tears because of a burdened heart which these children know their parents have wept on their behalf. A good example of this would be Monica, mother of St. Augustine.

God does not want us to be free of the burden or concern which we have for a lost loved one until that soul comes to Christ--even if we have to carry that burden to the grave with us. Often it is the witness for Christ which is left behind by some Christian who has gone home to be with Jesus which finally makes an impression on some lost soul, causing him to surrender his life to Jesus. God works in mysterious ways! What joy there will be in heaven when both parties meet there--the one who was burdened and the one who was lost.

Let me repeat: the non-Christian, as a rule, does not face this kind of deep sorrow. If a person is not concerned about his own soul's welfare, he is not likely to be concerned about the spiritual welfare of others. Some may want salvation for their children even when indifferent to their own souls' needs, when they do not want to depart from their wayward way of life. They may send their children to Sunday school and to church but seldom or never go themselves. The soul concern of such people usually does not go very deep.

5. God wants us to realize the sinful, wicked condition of this world and how the devil is gaining great victories in the war between good and evil. This, we can be sure, is depressing to God. He wills that true Christians share with Him in this concern. And this concern can be very depressing.

It isn't that the devil is more powerful than God. God could defeat the devil in one second if He willed to do so. This is not the problem.

The devil has his strength in his following. If no one willed to follow him and believe his lies, he would have no power.

And this is what is disheartening to God, that man wills to follow and believe Satan rather than his creator. And since this is man's choice, God, who has made us moral beings with the ability to choose whom we wish to follow, allows Satan to continue in his ways of evil.

God wills for His own to take the responsibility of making the truth about God's great love and saving grace known throughout this world, so that individuals can make the wise choice in following after

God and not after the world or after the ways of the devil. This then becomes a warfare between good and evil. War is known to have its own hardships and other aspects which are depressing. The Christian warfare is no exception.

6. God may burden us to take up some new and greater responsibility in the Christian warfare. Sometimes depression and fear overtake the Christian as he faces this new responsibility. This depression and fear could serve to help the Christian not to take his new responsibility lightly but to drive him to seek God's help through prayer. This could involve the burning of some bridges behind him, or to make some needed sacrifices. This is never easy; it is not done without a great deal of apprehension.

Nehemiah seemed quite contented and carefree as a cupbearer in the king's palace until God burdened him with the plight of His people in Jerusalem. Nehemiah then became deeply concerned and, I believe, even depressed because of the situation in Jerusalem.

7. There is a cost in being a Christian. God wants us to stand on certain convictions, based on the teachings of Christ. The world will ridicule and belittle the Christian for standing on such convictions. It might even persecute him for so doing. Such pressure will cause the Christian to have a heavy heart. He truly feels the heat of the battle, and this can be depressing.

But when he stands firm under such pressure and does not compromise with the world, he brings glory to God. "Blessed are they which are persecuted for righteousness' sake: for theirs is the kingdom of heaven. Blessed are ye, when men shall revile you, and persecute you, and shall say all manner of evil against you falsely, for my sake. Rejoice, and be exceeding glad: for great is your reward in heaven: for so persecuted they the prophets which were before you" (Matt. 5:10-12).

God will bring recognition and glory to Himself, causing others to follow and obey Him, as the result of the Christian's being persecuted.

8. The Bible says that we can best bring comfort and help to others who are suffering if we have experienced that same type of suffering (II Cor. 1:4). We can best help others who are depressed if we have experienced depression ourselves. It is only then that we can truly understand what they are going through. Jesus drank the full cup of suffering and well knows what every type of suffering is like, including depression. Therefore, He is able to feel with us in our suffering. It seems that it was necessary for Jesus to suffer as He did. If so, it becomes necessary for us to suffer if we want to be effective witnesses for Christ, to be able to identify with those who are suffering.

9. Depression helps us to realize our own limitations and our total dependency on God.

Some would maintain that it is a happy face with a smile that God can best use in winning the lost. I am sure He does use smiling faces, but there is no Scriptural basis for assuming that He always prefers a smiling face. There are many things in this world that sadden the Christian and should sadden him and even bring him to tears. God has use for such tears. The Christian does not suffer in vain.

Paul said, "For when I am weak (or saddened or helpless) then I am strong" (II Cor. 12:10). Often it is when we feel the most inadequate because of storm and testings, tried to the limit, that God uses us to bring credit and glory to Himself or to cause some soul to surrender his will to coincide with God's will for him.

God would want us to be honest with our feelings. We are not to pretend that we are happy when we are not. To be unhappy because we are burdened for the world we are living in does not make us any less a Christian.

Jesus was honest with His feelings. The Bible tells us how sad and depressed He was at times because of how He was rejected. He did not pretend to be something He was not.

The Psalmist also speaks of his unhappy, despondent feelings. Psalms 69 and 70 are examples as well as Psalms 42 and 43.

4. Sin and Depression

Sin can cause depression. We cannot conclude that it is not a contributing factor. However it is far from true that sin is the only reason, as some would claim. This is especially true in the life of a Christian, for whom this book was written. For a Christian, whose sins have been forgiven, it may not be a contributing factor. It was not the reason that Job or Elijah were depressed.

When sin is confessed and dealt with, then God forgives and promises not to remember these sins any longer. He also wants us to forget them, and this is the reason that He wants us to confess them. We need confess them only once. God will do the rest. After that, they are to be forgotten by both God and the sinner, to be remembered no more. "I, even I, am he that blotteth out thy transgressions for mine own sake, and will not remember thy sins" (Isa, 43:25). "for I will forgive their iniquity, and I will remember their sin no more" (Jer. 31:34b).

However, if we are still plagued with guilt because of those same sins, it is the devil and not God who is reminding us of them. We need not pay any attention to such accusations. The true Christian, who knows that sin is deadly to his soul, is sometimes apt to take conviction for sin which has already been confessed and forgiven, or for things which are not sin, because the devil is accusing him. The non-Christian who still needs to confess and repent of his sin, and who loves his sin, is not accused by the devil.

Often the depressed Christian fears that some past sin, even though confessed, might be the cause of his depression. The devil would like for him to think so. These depressed Christians will search their lives in vain for some sin which they fear might be the cause of their depression.

They would even be glad if they could find some sin to confess which they would then confess, hoping that this would relieve them of their depression. But, like Job, they search in vain.

This does not mean that we are no longer sinners, nor that we will never need to face the consequences of our past sins. But if there has been confession and repentance, God will give us grace to face and endure the consequence of such past sins. When God deals with us because of sin, He does not keep us guessing. When we leave ourselves open to His cleansing and leading, He shows us all we need to know and all He wants us to know about our sinful past. He does not leave us floundering around, wondering what we should do. He has made it clear that we need only repent (desire to do and be different than we are) and confess those sins that we are aware of to God.

Therefore, if you are a Christian, and if you cannot readily see how your depression relates to some sin, you can conclude that sin is not the problem but that there is some other reason that God allows and is taking you through a period of depression (see previous chapter). Some believe, as did Job's friends, that depression is a sign of God's displeasure; but like Job's friends, they are wrong.

Now we have just said that if we are Christian the cause of depression, very likely, is not sin. However, we need to qualify this statement. Depression may be due, not to sin, but to a lack of maturity in some area of our life. It may be due to the lack of knowledge of how to cope with a certain stressful situation which we are facing.

But this statement, too, needs to be qualified. Depression, for the Christian, can be compared to a schooling through which God wills to teach us many things. Many times it is the mature Christian whom God trains in this school of depression. You see, as in the case of Job, God wants to perfet the mature Christian still more.

It is those whom God has used and who have some maturity that He will purge in order to bring them to greater maturity and use them in a still more complete way. "And every branch that beareth fruit, he purgeth it, that it may bring forth more fruit" (John 15:2b).

If we already had had the wisdom which we gained from an experience of depression, we might not have had to suffer depression. If I had known what I now know as the result of my experience with depression, I would have known how to cope with the stresses which depressed me. It is through depression that I learned how to avoid depression. Depression was a schooling for me. After I understood and knew what I was to do because of the circumstances which I faced, the depression left me.

However, we cannot conclude that even though we have reached a certain level of maturity and wisdom we will suffer no more depression. We never know when God is through teaching or training us.

Jesus, who was perfect, showed signs of being deeply depressed while on this earth. Some claim that Jesus was not depressed. But it depends on how we define "depression." I think of it as being an extremely sad feeling. I know of no other person besides Jesus who sweat great drops of blood as He did in the Garden of Gethsemane because of the agony of His soul.

Some think of depression as a weakness or a flaw in a person's makeup or personality. This may be true in some cases, as when sin is the cause of depression, especially in the life of a non-Christian. For example: a sin, like drunkenness, could cause depression and often does. But depression is not always the result of a weakness or a flaw in someone's personality. Because Jesus was perfect in every way, some have difficulty in believing that He could ever have been depressed.

However, although Jesus was perfect, He suffered as no other person has ever suffered. He experienced many, if not all, types of suffering, including depression. And because He personally experienced intense suffering, He is able to identify and feel with us in any kind of suffering we might be experiencing, including acute depression. "For we have not an high priest which cannot be touched with the feeling of our infirmities; but was in all points tempted like as we are, yet without sin. Let us therefore come boldly unto the throne of grace, that we may obtain mercy, and find grace to help in time of need" (Heb. 4:15,16).

I know of no greater suffering than acute or clinical depression. Jesus was heartbroken because He was rejected by those He loved. I truly believe that this was very depressing to Jesus.

As Christians, as long as we have a place in this sinful world, and are concerned along with God about winning the warfare against evil, we subject ourselves to depression.

We might think of our "undoneness," our lack of understanding, or our confusion as sin, and in a sense it is. Our undoneness is all a part of our sinful nature. We are not complete. We are born in ignorance and we cannot help that. We have to learn some things the hard way so that we will not forget them. God often takes us in a roundabout way while teaching us in order to impress His way and His truth upon our mind and heart.

Once God asked Jeremiah to travel for many days across a desert area from Judea to the Euphrates River, in order to make known and impress His will on Jeremiah (Jer. 13:1-9).

Now God does not deal with or teach all people in the same way. He has different teaching methods for different people, depending on just how He plans to use them. He trains them in the work He has for them, and this differs from person to person. Instead of God's asking you or me to make a long trip across desert terrain, He may take us through a period of depression or some other crisis experience in order to school us.

God does not hold us accountable for what we cannot help or do not know. Yes, He may put us through some pain for our own good in order that we might learn some hard lesson. The only time we need to be convicted of not knowing something we need to know is when we have had a chance to learn but have not taken advantage of that opportunity. And if it is God's will that depression or a mental breakdown be the method of learning, or the type of schooling by which He chooses to teach us (all for our good), who are we to question His method of teaching?

Why then should we think of depression or testing from God as bad, when He uses it for good? Depression, when suffered by a Christian, is not suffering in vain; it has a worthwhile purpose in God's total plan of building His kingdom here on earth.

But how about depression as it relates to the non-Christian? A lot of them are not depressed but fully enjoy their sinful way of life. They are on their way to hell and either don't know it or don't care. They often appear more relaxed and carefree than does the Christian.

But that is only until their sins catch up with them, or until they begin to realize the seriousness of living in sin and out of fellowship with God. They might suffer depression which is used by God to drive them to Christ and cause them to repent and confess their sins as God clearly reveals these to them.

It is the law of God which God uses to cause such persons to see their sins and to realize their need for Jesus. At this point, however, it is not the law which they need but the Gospel.

This is where Job's friends made a great mistake. It was not the law which Job needed when he was very depressed, but the good news of the Gospel. The law as given by Job's friends did not help Job in his depression but only made him feel worse.

In trying to help a non-Christian who is very depressed, consider that it may be because he is under the conviction of sin that he is depressed. In such a situation, more law is not the solution to his problems; the Gospel needs to be applied. He needs to find release from his deep guilt feelings.

Jesus said, "And I, if I be lifted up from the earth will draw all men unto me" (John 12:32). Jesus did not say that we should continually remind others of their sins.

However, man does need to see his sin. This is vital in obtaining salvation. But God may already, in His own way, have caused someone to see his sin. In that case it is the healing balm of the Gospel which is sorely needed.

On the other hand, the man who is quite comfortable living in his sin needs to realize his own plight, and the law needs to be fully applied.

When a person hires out to an employer, he is expected to give of himself and of his strength, even to the point of becoming tired and weary by nightfall.

A soldier in battle is expected to give of himself in the same way for his country.

Jesus expects the same from those who have given themselves in serving Him. It is no sin to become weary, tired or even depressed if we have become that way as the result of serving Jesus or taking our place in the Christian warfare. Jesus never said that following Him would be an easy way (Acts 14:22).

Some seem to think that a Christian should never become weary, discouraged, and especially not depressed. But I have found no place in the Bible where we are admonished to take conviction for such feelings. Rather, when this happens we are invited to come to Jesus for restoration and renewed hope.

Jesus very tenderly and compassionately, with no note of rebuke or scolding in His words, invites us to come to Him when He says: "Come unto me, all ye that labor and are heavy laden, and I will give you rest" (Matt, 11:28).

But note: it is to the laborer, not to the sluggard or the lazy Christian, that this invitation is given.

5. God Purges His Own

"And every branch that beareth fruit, he purgeth it, that it may bring forth more fruit" (John 15:2b).

There are three important truths in this verse which can be a great encouragement to the Christian who is facing trial, suffering or testing of some kind, which could be in the form of depression.

First, notice that the text says, "He purgeth." God purgeth! The purging is done by God, not by Satan as some would maintain. In order that good might prevail and God's purpose be realized, He wills that the Christian endure certain types of concern, suffering or testing. "We must through much tribulation enter into the kingdom of God" (Acts 14:22). God proves His own. He loves them, but He does not pamper them.

An outstanding example of this is God's testing of Abraham. Think of the worry and fear that Abraham might have faced when God told him to sacrifice his only son Isaac. However, perhaps Abraham had such faith and confidence in God that it didn't really worry him. He didn't hesitate to obey. In due time God released Abraham from such a painful task, but not until Abraham passed the test of faith and obedience.

But suppose God had not released Abraham from this testing or that He had caused Isaac to become critically ill and die, taking him to Himself in heaven. God would still have worked it out for good as promised in Romans 8:28. So it would have been, unless Abraham had failed in the testing. It would have been possible for Abraham to have failed, but he didn't.

It is possible for anyone who is tested by God to fail. Many do fail. The story is told of a young father who dedicated his life for fulltime service to God. But then his small son was suddenly killed, and the father was known to have said, "If this is how God is going to treat me, I am not going to serve Him." This father did not pass the testing.

God has been known to test His own by calling home a loved one who was still very young. God's testing is not an easy testing. Yet, although many do fail, we need not fail.

But let me re-emphasize, unlike the tests we take in school where we receive no help from the teacher while taking the test, God is always willing and ready to help us endure all of His testings, no matter how severe. God gives grace to endure if we want to endure and do not forsake Him in order to follow after the ways of the world.

In one parish I served, I conducted a funeral for a nine-year-old girl who died of leukemia. Several weeks later the father said to me, with tears in his eyes, "We miss our little girl, but at the same time we feel honored that God wanted her to be with Him in heaven." Here were a man and his wife who passed the test put on them by God.

God, not the devil, does the purging!

Second, the verse says, "And every branch that beareth fruit, He purgeth it." We notice here that the purging is done to the fruit-bearing branch (the Christian) and not to the thistle (the non-Christian). It is the mature Christian, the one who has already bore some fruit and who is of the greatest use to God, whom He will test. It is God's desire, and it should be ours too if we are Christian, to become ever more usable and capable of bearing more and better fruit. As God purges the mature

Christian, this is made possible.

There needs to be a willingness on our part, if we are growing Christians, to suffer purging for Christ's sake and for the sake of extending God's kingdom on earth. We fight a warfare against evil, and it is not an easy warfare. If we are to win, it will take our best. The best training, even a purging by God, becomes necessary. Victory is never realized without cost.

Now the ungodly might also suffer because of the way they are living in open sin. And they will suffer in an even greater way after physical death if they do not repent.

However, many worldly people do prosper and seem to live a comfortable life here on earth. God says they have their reward (Matt. 5:45b, 6:2, 5, 16). It seems that God in His mercy does allow many ungodly people to prosper and enjoy life here on earth to a degree, knowing it will be the only joy they will have since eternity for them will he in hell. Some may even conclude from this that it does not pay to be a Christian and live a godly life because the ungodly many times seem to enjoy life to the fullest here on earth, while the Christians are persecuted and ridiculed and often suffer many hardships, all for the cause of Christ.

This does not mean that it is a sin to prosper financially, if the prospering is done honestly. Abraham, Job and David are examples of godly men who prospered and were rich with material wealth. We should not forget, however, that what we have in our possession is not our own. It belongs to God. We are only stewards of all that we possess and we will be held accountable as to how we use or misuse it.

There is some suffering, a purging

type of suffering, which can be avoided on this earth if we choose not to follow Jesus all the way.

The Christian walk here on earth is not a bed of roses, but it is the only way to heaven. To continue on with Jesus, not holding back, involves the carrying of a cross, paying a price, facing the storm, bearing the heat of the battle, or fighting the Christian warfare.

The cost of suffering has not become any less in our day than in ages past. The cost does not go down as we become more mature. There always are new and dangerous areas to be conquered for Christ. Some of these areas have become strongholds of Satan, which he is not ready to relinquish without a struggle.

This purging type of suffering is never forced upon us. We can avoid it by avoiding the Christian warfare or by refusing to let God prepare us (or purge us) for battle. But Jesus asks us to bear it willingly as soldiers of the cross, as good soldiers willingly undergo hard training and then face the battle for their country.

This is not what many of the so-called "joy prophets" are saying and writing today. They picture the Christian life as a life of joy, as continuous bliss, a carefree existence. They claim that if you are not experiencing this as a Christian, there must be something wrong with your Christianity. The Christian book market is flooded with this kind of thinking. Such thinking is contrary to the teaching of our text verse (John 15:2b) in which God speaks of purging the fruit-bearing vine. It is contrary to the teachings of the Bible.

Third, the verse says, "that it may bring forth more fruit." Although we are sinners and have an old sinful nature within us, which is prone to sin even after we have become Christians, God's purpose in purging us is not always in order to convict us of sin, tear us down, or cleanse our lives. Rather, as this verse indicates, God's purpose in purging us is to mature us, build us up, and make us capable of producing more and better fruit, all to the glory of God.

This does not mean that God does not punish sin. The Bible clearly states that He does. But in the life of a Christian, whose sins have been forgiven, God may well have other reasons for causing us to suffer or be purged.

Suffering builds character, if we do not allow it to break us. Suffering will give us compassion for others who suffer, if we do not allow it to harden us. Suffering will make us more usable to God so that we can bear more and better fruit to the glory of Christ. Suffering prepares us for heaven and gives us a longing to be there. "Blessed be God, even the Father of our Lord Jesus Christ, the Father of mercies, and the God of all comfort; who comforteth us in all our tribulation, that we may be able to comfort them which are in any trouble, by the comfort wherewith we ourselves are comforted of God" (II Cor. 1:3,4).

Again, it is the Christian whom God has already used who is put to the test so that God might be able to use him in a still greater way. Oh, dear Christian, thank God if He considers you worthy to suffer for His name's sake in order that greater glory be given to His name! Let this be your comfort: that God is preparing you for greater use.

II. DEPRESSION AS IT RELATES TO OUR BODY

6. How Our Physical and Mental Systems Compare

God created each of us with both a physical and an emotional or mental system. And as various disorders can upset the normal functioning of our physical system, the same is true of our mental system. Depression or mental illness are ailments which affect our emotional system. (Depression can be classified as a mental illness since it relates to our thinking process.)

In making a comparison between these two systems, the physical and the mental, let us compare a broken arm, which is a physical problem, with acute depression, which relates to our mental makeup.

First, let us observe something about our arms. If we put them through a continuing exercise program, they will develop and become stronger. A newborn baby has to learn to use his arms. With continuing effort, he learns to use them in many different ways and they continue to gain in strength through usage.

But now suppose a heavy object falls on one or both arms and breaks them. This weakens the arms and limits their ability to function for a time. Or suppose that later in life the arms are exposed to many hours of heavy lifting day after day over a long period of time. Such continuous strain would also have an adverse effect on the arms.

Therefore, we see that both the proper amount of exercise and the proper amount of rest are needed to develop and strengthen the arms, whereas too much strain all at once or over a long period of time without enough rest can weaken or damage the arms.

We can conclude from this that a balance between exercise and rest is needed in order to develop the arms to their maximum strength and ability and also to maintain their health.

It is also true that the more the arms have developed, the more strain they can take before they break. The arms of an adult can take more strain and more heavy work then the arms of a baby can.

Now let us turn our attention to the emotional or mental system. What has just been said about the arms is also true of our emotional system. Emotional stress, like activity for the arms, can either strengthen or tear down our emotional or mental stability. A steady diet of stress, problems, anxieties and worries (if they do not come too fast and too hard,) will serve to strengthen our emotional stability. If these stresses do not come in too quick succession and are not too great for us to handle, we learn what needs to be done in handling or coping with them. We become ever more efficient and capable of handling greater loads of stress or problems as time goes on. An adult is able to weather more stress and strain than a child can.

Now, too much stress, or the wrong kind of stress, which the person has not yet learned how to deal with, can (like too much pressure on the arms) break that person down emotionally. When this happens, we say he is suffering from a nervous breakdown or severe depression.

Some people seem to have a higher tolerance or breaking point before becoming depressed than others. They can take more stress before breaking down, just as some arms are stronger than others. Psalm 103:14 reminds us that we are made of dust. Everyone has a limit as to how much stress he can take all at once.

Our heredity, our childhood, our past experience, our Christian training or the lack of it, all help determine our emotional stability for the present. Certain kinds of stresses, which we have not learned how to deal with, will break us down more quickly than those with which we have had some experience. Nor are we all alike. Certain stresses may break some people down yet serve to strengthen the emotional stability of others.

Scientific research tells us that some people break down emotionally or become acutely depressed more quickly than others because of an inherited chemical deficiency. Whether this has actually been proven I do not know. The tendency seems to be, when focusing on chemical deficiency as the cause, to treat the patient with drugs, whereas counseling, especially Christian counseling, is a better way to help the depressed. It will help him to find the answer which he needs in order to cope with the stress he is facing. Counseling may work more slowly than drugs, but in the long run it is better and more satisfying to the patient.

It seems that in many cases, when the drug therapy is suddenly stopped, the depression becomes more acute; whereas through counseling, if the solution to the stress can be found, this will help the healing of the depression. However, other stresses at a later time could bring on more depression.

Whether or not chemical deficiency relates to a person's depression, it is stress or circumstances which trigger the depression, causing it to manifest itself in the patient. If there is such a thing as chemical deficiency, it takes less stress to cause such a person to become depressed.

It is through experience with stress

that we learn how to cope with stress. A thorough knowledge of God's Word as well as experience in dealing with stress are the best medicines available to maintain mental health and cure depression.

Directly or indirectly, all our strength and ability comes from God, including our ability to overcome physical and emotional stress. I could not blink my eyelids if God did not give me the strength and ability to do so. God is the One who helps me to develop in strength and ability, but He uses physical and emotional strain and stress in order to accomplish this. In this way He gives me a part in maintaining or regaining my mental health as I apply myself and cooperate with Him.

Now, in the light of what has been said thus far about stress, we realize that stress and problems in life are not all bad. Like exercise for the body, stress helps to develop our emotional stability. Can you imagine what kind of a milktoast or spineless personality we would be if we never faced any stress in our entire lives?

I once raised some tomato plants from seed in the house during the winter. They did well and grew to be tall plants. They were completely sheltered from all severe outside weather. One spring day I carefully transplanted them outside. They could not stand even a slight wind; they soon withered and died. They were not conditioned for outdoor weather.

You and I would react the same way if we lived our entire lives in a sheltered way, free of all stress and problems, and then suddenly came face to face with life as it really is. We would panic and collapse emotionally.

I have been told that when an arm, for example, is broken and then heals, the

- 37 -

arm bone is afterward strongest at the point of the break. In the same way, an emotional breakdown can and often does serve to strengthen a person emotionally. Like any other stress, once we have gone through a breakdown, it can help us better cope in the future with the particular type of stress which led to the breakdown.

As I look back at my own acute depression, I can realize much better now what the main cause of the breakdown was. I know that I am now much more capable of handling that type of stress than I was before I broke down.

We may be somewhat able to control the physical strain we put on an arm or leg. It is not so easy to control our stresses and problems and keep them from coming in upon us too fast. They just keep coming! However, there are certain things we can do.

First, we can try to face these stresses calmly and carefully, examining them one by one to see if there is anything we can do to solve these problems. Second, we can learn to live, as best we know how, so as to avoid as much stress as possible. Third, and most important of all, we can put our lives into the hands of God and seek His guidance in facing all of life's many problems. (More will be said about how to cope with stress and depression in Part III.)

God, who knows all things, knows how stress plays a part in maturing us and giving us emotional stability and strength. Therefore, He not only allows but even wants us to have some problems and storms in life. In Jesus' parable of the wise man and the foolish man, we are told that storms will come (Matt. 7:24-27). It was God who severely tested Job, a righteous man (Job 2:3).

If you are a Christian, God wants to use you in fighting the Christian warfare against evil and all that is satanic. We cannot expect Him to exempt us from that warfare, or expect the testings or training for that warfare to be light. Stress and testings by God serve to train and condition us for that warfare.

It is God's will that you bring comfort and help to others who are being tested. It becomes necessary for God to prepare you for such a ministry by leading you through some experiences of suffering. when we have experienced stress, depression or an emotional breakdown we will be better able to sympathize, show love and concern, and give help and advice to others who are facing a similar crisis. And we need not despair, because God's grace is sufficient (II Cor. 1:3-4).

As a Christian, and because of stress throughout our lives, we will be able to look back at the time of our death and realize how God has been with us and helped us through countless stressful situations. This will give us faith that God will help us when we face our last enemy death, and enable us to overcome it. ·The God who has never failed us will not fail us when we face physical death. As Christians trained in the school of stressful situations and depression, we can be used by God to help others prepare for and face death.

God has promised heaven to Christians. However, He has not promised heaven on earth. In heaven we will be free of all stress and worry, having graduated from the same. Here again, let me repeat: God loves us but He does not pamper us. He wants us to grow up and be adults. Stress, problems in life, and the like are used by God to help us grow and mature as Christians. Let us learn to accept these things and not fight against them or imagine them to be otherwise. God in His wisdom knows best. He has promised to turn all things into good for those who are His beloved children (Rom. 8:28).

7. Self-pity and Living in Regret

There are those who claim that self-pity is the cause of all depression, and that if the depressed person will stop feeling sorry for himself he will be cured of his depression. This is not true, and it could be a dangerous thing to say to a depressed person. It will cause him to be more confused, take on more guilt, and become more depressed.

Let us again look at our physical being and make a comparison between the emotional illness of depression and an open wound which is physical. Both the open wound and depression are caused by circumstances or situations outside ourselves. Health problems could be an exception. However, with many health problems it is likewise something outside the person which is the cause.

Self-pity is to depression what an infection is to an open wound. In both cases, it is not the cause, but its infection will slow the healing process. Self-pity, like an infection, is dangerous. It can be more acute in some than in others.

It is much more difficult to give encouragement, or to get the depressed person to take encouragement, where there is self-pity. It causes the depressed individual to want to give up, to give in to his feelings of listlessness and to remain idle. He lacks the ambition to carry on or to try again. Often, those who are afflicted with self-pity refuse to cooperate with treatment or with those who want to help them. They have a defeatist attitude and think, "Oh, what is the use." Extreme self-pity can lead to suicide.

But let us not be too quick to judge those who are filled with self-pity. Love and sympathy to the depressed are like cleansing to an open wound. Just as cleansing can prevent infection, love and sympathy can prevent self-pity and decrease the possibility of depression.

We know that if dirt and bacteria enter the wound, the chance of infection is greatly increased. In like manner, if a person lives in a situation, perhaps from early childhood, where little love, understanding and encouragement are given, depression, infected with self-pity, is much more likely to occur.

It is questionable whether anyone can live entirely free of self-pity when he receives little or no love and encouragement. I fear that any of us would sooner or later become a helpless victim of self-pity where there is no love present. Christian love and understanding keep the wound of depression clean so that the infection of self-pity cannot enter.

If the person is not a Christian and does not know of the love of Christ, the danger of self-pity is more acute. Jesus wills to channel His love through Christians who are willing to love, sympathize, give encouragement and share God's Word. This tells of Jesus' great love for sinners with problems.

There is little that anyone can do for a person who insists on wallowing in self-pity. He can be a discouragement to a friend or loved one who wants to help him. He needs to be willing to let go of his self-pity and reach out for the love which others are offering to give. The break-through in such a situation is to get the afflicted person to see his own potential and become involved in doing for himself what he can, looking to Jesus to help him. (See chapter entitled: "Do Not Be Idle--Get Involved").

We should never stop loving a person who is depressed and afflicted with self-pity, but stern discipline may be needed to get the person to stop feeling sorry for himself and become involved in his own healing. When he shows signs of doing this, be quick to praise him and encourage him. He may slip back again; like a dry pump, he may need to be primed with encouragement and whatever discipline is needed. He needs to realize that self-pity only hinders healing.

A twin to self-pity is "living in regret." It, too, hinders the healing of depression. We cannot change the past, but we can pick up the pieces left over from past mistakes and go on.

Living in regret can be mistaken for repentance or the confession of sin. The difference is that true repentance and confession of sin need only be done once for any particular sin; then it is to be forgotten by both God and the sinner. But the person who lives in regret will continuously dwell on past mistakes and sins, refusing to forget them and go on with his life.

The person who lives in regret feels sorry for himself, believing that he has blundered so badly that it is useless for him still to try to make something of his life. He lacks the ambition to try again. He refuses to be encouraged or take hope for the future. He may have certain talents, like playing the piano or the ability to make things with his hands, yet refuse to make use of these talents again. He will readily talk of past successes and of what he once achieved with his talents, yet feel that it would be useless for him to take up his talents again.

Such a person needs to be made to realize that with Jesus there is no dead-end road. Jesus will always forgive our sins and past mistakes as we confess them, and readily gives new strength and wisdom to start over. We learn from past mistakes. Our lives may seem hopeless and dashed to bits, but if we do not give up, Jesus will help us put them back together again and make something out of them. It is never too late to try again. Our lives may never again be what they once were, or what we at one time hoped they would be, but a great peace can be ours if we look to Jesus, continue to do our best with what we have, and press on.

The person living in self-pity and regret needs to be assured that there is no sin or mistake that God will not forgive the repentant sinner, and that the sins of the past need not haunt our present and future. But we must flee the sin of idleness and keep on trying.

"If we confess our sins, he is faithful and just to forgive us our sins and to cleanse us from all unrighteousness" (I John 1:9). Also see Hebrews 8:12 and 10:17.

8. Confusion

We know that stress and excessive worry which cause depression can hinder the patient's ability to concentrate and make decisions. As I write this, I draw upon my own experience of losing my ability to concentrate for a limited time. I think back into this experience and remember what my feelings and thinking were at the time. I realize that my knowledge on this subject is limited. There may be aspects of the problem which scientific research has discovered of which I am not aware. I share my thoughts on this for whatever they might be worth to others.

The feeling of depression and lack of ability to concentrate and make decisions are very closely related. The depression causes the other two symptoms. The fact that the patient is not able to think and reason as he once was able to do, terrifies him and adds to his depression. He realizes that his mental abilities are not what they once were, and he wonders if he is going insane.

The feeling is like trying to put a jigsaw puzzle together to get a clear picture but not being able to find all the pieces. Or it is like trying to get a clear picture on a worn-out television set. Everything seems out of focus. And because the acutely depressed person cannot clearly think through what he is trying to concentrate on and get a clear picture of all the facts as they relate to each other, he feels inadequate to make a wise decision on the matter.

Even little things like trying to figure out what clothes to wear, whether to eat dark or white bread, or to take a bath can become major problems, causing much worry and take up a great deal of his thinking.

In the mentally healthy person, there seems to be a signal like a green light which will give him the go-ahead to act on a decision he has been pondering. If he doesn't get the green light he hesitates. For the extremely depressed, even in simple matters such as what to wear, the green light doesn't seen to come on. He lacks the freedom to act or go ahead.

The healthy person makes many decisions quite naturally and almost automatically. He doesn't need to give them a whole lot of thought. The green light is working.

In the more complicated problems or the making of decisions, like whether to look for a different job or buy a home, the green light does not come on so quickly. We find it best to ponder the facts for a while before making a decision too hastily.

Sometimes, because something appeals to us, we might go against the green light and against our better judgment, only to regret the decision we made. We begin to worry about the final outcome, and it may seem like a great loss to us, but all is not lost. We do learn through such an experience which causes us to move forward more cautiously in the future.

It would seem that the bulb in the green light has burned out in the person whom depression makes unable to concentrate. It does not light up when it should. It could be because the depressed person went against the warning of the red light at one time and that he has become overly cautious, he doesn't trust the green light and feels safer with a red light being his guide. A balance needs to be maintained between being overly cautious and not being cautious enough.

We may see the person whose green light has gone out sitting in one position for a long time, just staring at the floor with a blank look on his face. He is unable to make the decisions needed in order to continue on. Many thoughts may be racing through his mind which are unrelated to that which he needs to concentrate on at the moment in order to reach a decision. The person seems to have little or no control over which thoughts are to occupy his thinking process at present. His mind wanders. At least, this was my experience when I was very depressed.

Such a person may spend hours trying to decide which pair of shoes to buy, or wonder if he should buy shoes at all. In the end, rather than make a decision, he will look to someone else, if he can find such a person, to make the decision for him.

We can best help such a person by encouraging him to take the risk of making his own decisions--especially decisions which are not too costly or overly risky.

The mentally healthy person knows how to plan his day. We say that he has his wits about him. He is able to take hold of what information is needed and think it through and come to a decision. The confused, depressed person does not seem to have his wits about him and seems unable to think logically.

Any kind of decision-making becomes a very fearful thing to the acutely depressed person. For this reason he fears going anywhere and prefers staying at home where life is less complicated. He feels listless and tired, and that he is forever going against the red light because he sees no green light. If he makes a decision, he tends to want to go back to the position of indecision because he fears the outcome.

Therefore, he remains in a constant state of confusion. He is unable to function and do the things he normally did. He cannot figure out what steps he should take and in what order he is to take them.

He may begin to question his entire life and wonder if he ever made a right decision or did anything right. He may even regret the decisions he made a long time before. His moral life comes into the picture. If he is a Christian and has lived a clean, moral life, he may wonder if he has needlessly denied himself certain pleasures which he previously thought to be sinful. He may wonder if this might be the cause of his depression. At the same time, his conscience may bother him because of things which he now questions as being permissible for a Christian. He wonders if God might not be punishing him with depression because of something he did in the past. He may wish that he had never been born.

Any person may come to a crossroad in life and not know which way to go, He may spend a lot of time pondering the facts which relate to making a decision. Until the green light comes on, he may be confused, and this confusion may make him depressed.

Or he may face a situation in which he does not know what to do, but then through the wise counsel of others or new thoughts which have come to him, he is able to figure out what to do. The green light finally comes on and the confusion and depression disappear. However with the deeply depressed, the green light never seems to come on.

I do not know all the reasons which would cause a person to become so depressed that he loses his ability to concentrate and make decisions. Scientific research indicates that it could be hereditary. But I believe that there are also other causes. Again I speak only from my own experience.

To go against one's own conscience or better judgment is bad for one's mental health. Or, to suddenly do something or say something which previously he had no freedom to say or do could cause, I believe, a lot of worry and a loss of concentration ability. I heard of a man who was found wandering around at a race track all confused and completely mute. He was taken to a state hospital where later it was discovered that he had gambled and lost everything he had at the races.

I remember that when I was in the army during World War II, I wrote a letter to my father in which I stated some things which later I greatly regretted and which caused me a great deal of worry. In this letter I questioned my father's Christianity. I was afraid that I had offended him. At the time that I wrote it, I reasoned that it would be for my father's own good and that God wanted me to do this. I now believe that it must have been the devil who was pushing me. I also tempted God by praying: "If sending this letter is not pleasing to you, do not let this letter ever reach my father." But my father received the letter. He never answered it.

It was totally unlike me to write and send this kind of letter. I acted completely against my better judgment. I feared that it might sever the relationship which I had with my father. Up to that time I had been looking forward to going home after the war, but now I began dreading going home and facing my father. I could not stop worrying about it. I thought of writing another letter to apologize to Dad. But I feared that would only complicate the situation. What was done was done. There didn't seem to be any way that I could undo what I had done.

A short time later I discovered that

I was becoming very forgetful. After getting up and washing and shaving in the morning I would forget reveille (roll call) which was expected of me as a soldier. Instead I would go back and sit on my bed. Sometimes I would just sit there for a long time while my mind wandered with all kind of thoughts and worries, and miss my breakfast. I would forget to go to meals. I became totally confused in trying to write letters, not being able to concentrate on one thought or one incident long enough to describe it completely. I finally went on sick call, spent several months in a hospital, and was given an honorable discharge. There were other factors which entered into the cause of my breakdown, but going against my better judgment in the kind of letter I wrote to my father was a major factor.

It turned out that my father was much wiser, more understanding and forgiving than I had ever imagined. When I came home he welcomed me with open arms as if nothing had ever come between us. Only once was the letter mentioned, when I apologized for having written it, which was shortly after coming home. There was no need that it be mentioned again. It never haunted me after that.

Another factor which can cause this kind of confused depression with a loss of ability to concentrate is to be caught between two conflicting loyalties, such as having two girl friends and not knowing how to cut the relationship with either one as the courtships thicken.

Another example is to belong to a church or group which is not teaching as you believe. You may feel that you should withdraw, but you love the fellowship, having had close fellowship with several others who belong. In such a dilemma you do not know whether you should give your full support and loyalty or to withhold. And as long as you remain in the fellowship you may feel that you owe it your full support and loyalty, but doing so troubles your conscience.

Still another example could be that of a wife living with an alcoholic husband. She does not know whether she should live with him, take his abuse, and continue to be a Christian witness to him, or to leave him.

And it might be that the person knows what he should do but lacks the courage to go through with it. He may not be willing to pay the price that the right decision would demand. Sometimes doing the right thing from a Christian standpoint might not only cost money but also friends and reputation, or something else which is very dear.

The situation which causes the confusion may cause one to become bitter toward certain other people or even against the whole world, assuming that the whole world is against him and is the cause of his problem. We call this being paranoid. In his confusion he may think of those who befriend him as his enemies. Such a person may imagine that others are plotting against him.

A person so affected often does not know the cause or all of the contributing factors responsible for his confusion and depression. There could be more than one cause, or there could be some minor causes, along with a major cause.

If a person has trouble making little decisions, it might be that at some time in the past he failed to make a proper major decision which has been pushed back into the sub-conscious mind. However, it is blocking the way for any further decision-making and needs to be dealt with before this individual can again be himself. When this person can clearly see what he should have done, face it, and still do what can be done about it (apologize to some one or whatever), healing will follow. It is like seeing a green light and moving forward again.

Sometimes the cause or key to unlocking the depression will lie buried deep in the sub-conscious mind. It could have been there for years. It may not be easy to find or uncover but, if found and dealt with, mental health will be more quickly restored.

However, even if the causes are not discovered, the illness may still eventually be cured. In most cases it will run its course, first doing damage to the mental health but then finally no longer consciously or subconsciously haunting the individual. Time has a way of eventually healing.

In extreme cases the damage could become permanent and the person may continue to deteriorate mentally, never becoming his old self again. The problem seems to be lodged deep in the sub-conscious mind and continues to have a damaging effect upon the patient.

I was once told of a case in which a fisherman was in a shipwreck during a storm at sea. He saw a drowning man who pleaded with him to save him. But the man was almost immediately swept out to sea by the storm and drowned. This incident lay buried in the sub-conscious of the fisherman for years and continued to haunt him. He felt guilty for not trying to save the man.

Finally the incident was brought into conscious realization and this fisherman could see that there was nothing that he could have done to save the man, and the incident no longer haunted him,

There is the paranoid person who is confused and who has an exaggerated degree of self-love. He believes that others act hostile and persecute him. Such people are less apt to become depressed, because they blame others for their problems. Their conscience is free and they are able to live with themselves. However such a person often lives a very lonely life, believing everyone to be out-of- step but himself. (There will be more about the paranoid in chapter 27).

There is, however, always a right answer or a right decision which should be made. It might not be easy to find; and it may be costly or difficult to follow through on. But God knows the right answer and will help us to find it and do what should be done. Becoming more and more acquainted with His word, the Bible, and looking to God in prayer will help us know and do what ought to be done. And He will give us the courage and strength to do what is right, and He will go with us, or Jesus will go with us, as we face the consequence of our decisions.

Christian fellowship and counsel from wise Christian friends who understand the situation can be of great help to the confused depressed person in gaining the wisdom he needs for the problems he faces.

"If any of you lack wisdom, let him ask of God, that giveth to all men liberally, and upbraideth not; and it shall be given him. But let him ask in faith, nothing wavering. For he that wavereth is like a wave of the sea driven with the wind and tossed" (James 1:5-6).

9. The Weary Christian Warrior

In speaking of discouragement we need to define the term. To be discouraged is to be sad, perhaps extremely sad. Some seem to associate discouragement with "giving up" or allowing oneself to be tempted to give up.

It has become disgraceful for a Christian to become discouraged in our day. It is often thought of as a sin. But if discouragement is a sin, it is different from any other sin. Sin appeals to our sinful, selfish nature, and it is this appeal which tempts us to participate. The sin itself promises and gives a certain amount of pleasure and satisfaction for the moment. It is the end result of sin which is so damaging to the soul.

But discouragement appeals to no part of man, including his old nature or new--if he is a Christian. No one wills to be discouraged.

It is the circumstances around man, or the situation he finds himself in, which causes a person to become discouraged. It invades him like an enemy and he has no power to resist. It engulfs him like a flood, often suddenly and without warning. It invades him from the outside rather than tempting him from the inside.

Yet there are those who would admonish the Christian when he is discouraged, as if he willed it so or brought it upon himself. They think of all discouragement as a flaw in one's faith, or as letting Satan or some demonic force assail him and take away his Christian joy or peace. This is like rubbing salt into the wounds of the bleeding person.

Because of these lies about discouragement, which are of the devil and not of God, there are many who have come

- 54 -

to believe that there is something wrong with them and their faith in God when trying circumstances discourage them.

Unless we have been living in sin, which can cause discouragement, we need not be ashamed of discouragement. Many Christians become discouraged in fighting the Christian warfare which is never an easy warfare.

There are those who claim to have a quick cure for all discouragement. "Just have faith in God," they say. "If you have faith in God you should not be discouraged." Or they quote a few of their favorite Bible verses, often out of context; and if this does not bring a quick cure, they conclude that there must be something radically wrong with the person who is discouraged. The fault, according to them, is always in the one discouraged, never in the method being prescribed.

The end result of such a quick prescribed cure only causes the discouraged person to become more discouraged and depressed. He feels more than ever that God has deserted him or that he is being punished for some sin when he has no knowledge of what the sin might be and very likely never committed.

But God has His reason for allowing and even leading the Christian through the valley of discouragement. He has something to teach us or impress upon us--a quick cure does not allow time for such teaching.

Those who advocate such a quick cure for all discouragement remind me of the Pool of Bethesda (John 5:1-9) which seemed to promise healing to many but actually helped only a very few.

We live in a world of sin with much that is not according to God's will. There are discouraging circumstances all around us which affect each of us in different ways. This is only natural, not sinful. Since the Christian has feelings he too is affected.

In studying our Bible we see godly individuals who became discouraged. God did not rebuke them for being discouraged, but met them in love and gave encouragement and hope.

Some of David's psalms describe his discouragement with which he was plagued at certain times. (Psalms 42, 43, 44). Naomi was so discouraged that she felt that God had deserted her (Ruth 1:13). Nehemiah was so heavy-hearted that even the king noticed it (Neh. 1:4-2:2). Because of the ungodly circumstances around him, Jeremiah became known as the weeping prophet. In the New Testament, Paul revealed how discouraged he was at times, in his Corinthian and Galatian letters. Jesus, who knew no sin, was discouraged because He was rejected by the world as its Savior from sin. His love for the world was met with hate.

We can best help the discouraged if we view discouragement in its true form. When Jesus says, "Let not your heart be troubled" (John 14:1), He is not rebuking those who have a troubled heart. He is assuring us that He has the situation under control and that He can give hope in a discouraging situation. He tends to heal the discouragement we feel rather than chastening us for it.

We do well to admit it, first to ourselves but also to others, when we are discouraged. Like Jesus, we do well to be honest with our feelings and not pretend that all is well when it is not.

However, to become discouraged is not the same as giving up or abandoning all hope. To give up is the easy way out and could be classified as a weakness and in some cases as a sin.

Discouragement should drive us to prayer and to God's Word, looking for a solution to our predicament. If discouragement does only this for us, it will have served a useful purpose. But allowing discouragement to completely defeat us, stagnate our efforts, and to give up all hope will have an ill or even devastating effect upon us.

In our discouragement we need to learn to exercise patience, especially patience with God. God will not forget His own and in His good time will work it all out for good (Rom. 8:28). (see chapter 16, "Waiting on God".

As Christians, in the midst of the Christian warfare, we are prone to become discouraged. This is not a sin. When we have Jesus as our Lord and Saviour we need never panic. We can always be assured that Jesus has the situation well in hand and that He will never let it get out of His control. If our problems should be with us until we reach our grave (if God should so will it for some reason), we can take hope that in heaven these problems will be removed (Ps 37:23-24).

In Jesus' parable, "The Laborers in the Vineyard" (Matt. 20:1-16), Jesus compares following Him to working for Him. Isn't that what is expected of us as we go into the world as His witnesses?

A worthy employee begins the day after a good night's rest, refreshed and ready to do what his employer expects of him. During the day he spends the energy he has stored up in himself.

When the day is done or evening comes, he is tired and weary. He needs a rest. But this is what is expected of him, and this is what this employee agreed to do for a wage.

In the same way the Christian is expected to give himself as he follows Jesus. He spends himself for Jesus because he loves Jesus and because of the hope of heaven which Jesus has promised to those who faithfully follow and serve Him.

But then as he gets tired, weary, discouraged and even depressed in such giving of himself, Jesus invites him to come to Him for restoration. "Come unto me, all ye that labor and are heavy laden," says Jesus, "and I will give you rest."

Notice that it is those who have labored or worked (those who are out in the world witnessing for Jesus) and those who are heavy laden or discouraged and depressed that Jesus invites to come.

But then, when we come to Jesus, He will take our burden, the work we are doing for Him, so we can rest. We can leave it all with Him.

And when we come to Jesus in need of rest, we learn to work with Him and to leave what we can't handle for Him to take care of. We learn from Jesus! He will teach us how to do what is expected of us with greater ease, so as not to tire so quickly. This, I believe is what Jesus is telling us when He says, "For my yoke is easy, and my burden is light" (Matt.11:30).

Nevertheless, this doesn't change our responsibility to Jesus. We are still, if Christian, expected to give ourselves willingly for His cause.

III. WHAT TO DO WHEN DEPRESSED

10. Waiting on the Lord

"Wait on the Lord, be of good courage, and He shall strengthen thine heart: Wait, I say, on the Lord" (Psalm 27:14).

Jesus is the master in dealing with depression. We act wisely and do well if we learn and cooperate with Him in dealing with our own depression or in ministering to someone who is depressed.

There are a number of practical things that we can do to overcome depression and maintain mental health. I speak of these later in this book. The first and most important thing we can do is "wait on the Lord." It is basic. The other points which I make are only suggestions that one can try. Even if we fail in these there is still hope. God in His mercy may still heal, even if we don't do these things. However, to wait on Him is most essential.

Notice that the above verse does not say, "Have faith in God," "Trust in the Lord," or "Believe on the Lord." I believe there is a difference between "having faith," "trusting" and "believing" and just simply "waiting." In this verse God simply asks that we "wait on Him." Faith which is essential for salvation will come later. To begin with, we are to "wait on the Lord" as we give ourselves to the prayerful study and meditation of His Word.

Now what does it mean to wait? And why are we to wait? To wait is not the same as being idle. We are to wait on the Lord as a student would wait on his teacher to impart knowledge, guidance, skills and whatever help a teacher is capable of giving.

Now, a teacher usually uses a text book; so does our Lord. The text book is the Bible--God's Word to us. The Holy

Spirit teaches the same truth which Jesus taught His disciples (John 14:17,26), and He teaches in conjunction with God's Word. He teaches what the Bible teaches and never anything different.

In a good student-teacher relationship, there is communication as the student asks questions and seeks guidance from the teacher. In our relationship with our Lord or the Holy Spirit, we call such communication prayer. As we read, study, listen to and meditate on God's Word, we need to do it in the spirit of prayer.

As we wait on the Lord (or Holy Spirit) to be taught and led, He will not only help us to understand the Word of God and give us help or grace to apply it to our lives, but He will also convince us of its truth and dependability.

And when we are convinced that God's Word is true and dependable, we have faith--faith to trust Jesus with our very life, as He asks us to turn it over to Him for cleansing and re-shaping. Faith, therefore, is something which comes from God, and which He works into our life; but it all begins by our "waiting on the Lord or the Holy Spirit" and our willingness to be taught and led by Him.

I have come to realize, especially as the result of my experience with depression and mental illness, that it truly is as Martin Luther says in his explanation of the third article in his "Small Catechism." He says: "I cannot by my own reason or strength believe in Jesus Christ my Lord or come to Him." By myself, within the limits of my own ability, I find that I cannot trust or have faith in God, but I can wait on Him as He teaches me what I must do if I am to receive a saving faith in Jesus, "So faith comes by hearing, and hearing by the Word of God" (Romans 10:17).

It is easy for a preacher or writer to say to a lost soul or a Christian in distress, "Just believe, just have faith in God." It sounds so very simple, but the impossible is often being asked.

We live by faith, but unless God first reveals Himself to us in some way, through answered prayer, some experience in life, and most important of all, through His Word, we can no more believe or have faith in Him than we can fly. But we can wait on Him!

I am very dependent on God for everything. I cannot even blink an eyelid until He gives me the strength to do it. And I cannot have faith to believe in Him unless He first, in some way, proves to me that He is trustworthy. But I can wait on Him.

If God is putting me through some kind of testing, like He did to Job (the book of Job), or as He sometimes does to people; or seems to be hiding Himself from me for a period of time, or doesn't come to my rescue as soon as I would wish Him to do; then I find it hard, or harder, to trust Him, believe in His promises, and have faith in Him. The testings could cause my faith to weaken, or I could lose faith altogether. If so, I cannot regain that faith again by my own efforts. But I can still wait on Him.

However, God knows how impossible it is for us to have faith in Him, especially when put to the test. He knows that we cannot gain a faith with our own strength or ability. God does not expect the impossible! "For He knoweth our frame; He remembereth that we are dust" (Psalm 103:14). He does not condemn us for having a weak faith, especially if tested.

God did not judge me or condemn me because of my doubts and almost complete loss of faith in Him when I was severely tested with acute depression while in a mental hospital. Again, I refer you to my book, "My Experience with Clinical Depression".

It is as Jesus said about Himself in Matthew 12:20: "A bruised reed shall He not break, and smoking flax shall He not quench." Isaiah also said this about Jesus many years earlier (Isa. 42:3).

In other words our faith may become bruised to the point of falling apart, like a bruised reed. Or it may lose its fire like flax straw which once was aflame but now is only smoking. God may, by testing us, allow our faith almost to die; but He does not let it die if we continue to wait on Him, if we do not willingly reject Him by following the ways of sin and the world, and if we do not completely give up.

In due time God will again strengthen our faith like a bruised reed which mends and again is strong. And He will, in due time, reveal Himself to us that our faith may again be aflame like burning flax straw as it once was or more so.

It is as these text verses promise: if we wait on Him He will strengthen our heart; He will give us a will to press on; He will work faith in our life. But all of this is God's doing and not our own. Our part is to continue to wait on Him, wait on Him as a student waits on his teacher. When God tests us, He takes from us rather than giving or blessing us in some way we would desire. He may test us to see how much we love Him or whether we will remain faithful and wait on Him.

God tested Abraham, whom He greatly loved. He asked him to sacrifice his only son Isaac. He put Job, Joseph, Daniel, and other great men of Bible history through great testings. It was their remaining faithful in the midst of these testings which made them great and pleasing to God.

God may test you and me. We can expect the same from God. If we just wait on Him, even when our faith is weak, the end result will be a stronger faith than ever. God does not forsake those who remain true to Him through the storm. The end result of my testing in the way of acute depression and time in a mental hospital was a stronger faith in God, a greater assurance that He is, His Word is true and dependable, and He has an inheritance in heaven waiting for me. This assurance came after I had gone through a time of great doubt and confusion.

Therefore, dear reader, let me urge you to "wait on the Lord." Wait on the Lord as an attentive student waits on his teacher and as God teaches you through His Word. Wait on God even when you are not sure about God, when He seems far away, and even when it seems as if He has deserted you.

I did not know where God was when I was severely tested. I could not understand why He allowed me to be placed in a mental hospital when all my life I had had a desire to obey His commandments and to serve Him. I wanted to bring honor to His name and to learn what He had to teach me. If there was a God, why did He allow this to happen to me?

But I had seen enough of the world to know that there was no future in living for the world, because I knew the world certainly had nothing to offer. Perhaps one could enjoy the pleasures of the world for a season, but that death comes later was very evident to me. Death was out there waiting for everyone, and I knew it was waiting for me.

Since death was staring me in the face,

of what value was a short fling of pleasure in the world? The pleasures of the world were not appealing in a mental hospital. What was there to do but to wait on the Lord? God still was my only hope, even though my faith in Him was weak, because there was no hope in anything else.

Therefore, I was determined to be faithful in all my Christian convictions and not willfully sin or bring discredit to my Lord, no matter what happened to me. Even though it seemed as though God had deserted me, I would not desert Him--no matter what.

I would continue to wait for a better day, even with little assurance or hope within myself that there ever would be a better day. I would not give up! I would not take my own life or willfully do anything to harm either my body or soul. I did not know how I could stand the depression much longer, but somehow I seemed to be standing it. I would just wait and continue on in my depression as long as it plagued me, even if it killed me as I was afraid that it might.

My experience with depression was like waiting out in the cold, late at night and late in the season, for a bus, not being at all sure that the bus was still running. But since it was too far to walk to the place I hoped to go, if I did start to walk I would miss the bus--if there was a bus running. My only hope was to wait for that very uncertain bus. And so I wait, and I would wait all night if need be, because there was nothing else I could do.

Sometimes all that one can do is to wait on God when you are not at all sure He is anywhere near or if He even hears you when you pray.

In my case I found that the bus was still running. In due time, when the depression had accomplished what God purposed for it to accomplish in my life, He lifted the depression.

The whole experience was a schooling for me with God as my teacher. I learned much about life and about God through this experience. The value received in the schooling of depression far outweighed the cost in suffering. God worked it all out for good. He did strengthen my heart as He had promised to do if I would wait on Him.

We tend to become impatient whenever we face a time of crisis or suffering in our lives. When we bring the matter to God in prayer, our one concern is to pass through this crisis and be relieved of the suffering just as soon as possible. We would like God to do a miracle at once so that the crisis might pass and be gone, never to plague us again. We might even feel that if God worked such a miracle for us, we could tell the whole world about it, and this would bring great honor to God and He would be very pleased.

But if God worked such a miracle immediately, we would miss much of the schooling and much of the blessing He wants us to gain from the crisis situation. God is not nearly as anxious to be known as a great miracle worker as we might think. He is much more interested in saving souls. He gave his very best, His only begotten Son, in order that we might be saved.

Often, when Jesus performed a miracle of healing, He asked those who witnessed it to tell no one. (Matt. 8:4; Mark 5:43; Mark 7:36; Luke 5:14; and Matt. 9:30.) But when He saved the soul of the Samaritan woman, He was pleased when she told the whole city of Sychar what He had done for her (John 4).

We are not able to go through any of

our secular schools for one day and hope to graduate. What kind of education would we have if we attended only one day of our life? We spend much time, hard work, and painful concentration in our secular school system, taking the tests required in preparing ourselves to live in this world. Should we then expect God to graduate us from the training He has for us in the school of suffering before He has had a chance to teach and train us properly for eternity and for that which He would will of us to do for Him and His cause while living our life here on this earth? "We must through much tribulation enter into the kingdom of God" (Acts 14:22).

We need to learn to be patient with God and be willing to continue in whatever school of suffering He wants us to go through. Such times are needful in order that we might be able to receive the full blessing, both temporal and eternal, which God intends for us.

God's school of suffering, like the secular school which involves years of our time, does have a time of graduation. With some people, and with some kinds of suffering, graduation comes with physical death. We don't completely graduate from all types of suffering and anxieties, when a Christian, until our time of physical death. Quite often, however, a particular type of suffering involves only a certain period of time in our earthly life. And we need to be willing to learn the lessons God wills to teach us through suffering. We need to be willing to suffer as long as God wills that we suffer. We need to pray for patience to endure when going through a period of suffering and not for a miracle of quick healing, so that we can realize the full training and blessing which God wants to give to us through our suffering. If Christian, we do not suffer in vain. Our final and greatest blessing will be heaven, where there is no suffering.

When depressed or facing a crisis, if you remember nothing else but to "wait on the Lord," you will be putting into practice the greatest and best cure for depression. Just resigning yourself to waiting on the Lord, no matter what, will, already, help you to endure, come what will. Live one moment at a time. Look to God to help you through each day. When faith is weak, when doubts come, nevertheless "wait on the Lord" as you prayerfully feed your soul on God's Word.

Also continuously feed your soul on the Word of God which you have stored in your heart. We may not always be able to read and concentrate on God's truth, as was my situation for a period of time, or we may not always be in a situation where we have access to a Bible; at such time feed your soul on that Word which you have stored in your mind and heart.

Wait on the Lord! Do not despair! Never give up! Giving up could lead to suicide! Continue to bear the suffering even when you feel you cannot bear it any longer. Remember that God knows your limitations. And He knows them much better than you do. He will give you grace (strength) for as long as you need it. But he gives it to us only a moment at a time.

And because God gives grace, we can endure much more pain, much more stress, much more suffering than we ever imagined--all to the glory of God.

As we imagine what it will be like in looking ahead to a stressful situation which we are facing and think of what is apt to be, we tend to panic. We so often think only of our limited resources and tend to forget God's grace which is available for the asking.

Some commit suicide at this point, not because the present moment is unbearable, but because they fear the future, which may not even be as they imagine. But as we continue on, waiting on the Lord, no one given moment is ever so unbearable that we cannot endure it. It may seem at times that we are going to sink, but somehow, as we continue to wait on the Lord, we soon discover that we are staying afloat.

When I was suffering from acute depression, there were times that I was afraid that I wouldn't be able to endure it for another minute. But somehow God enabled me to endure day after day, week after week and month after month. In due time, when the depression had accomplished God's will in my life, and when I had learned all He wanted me to learn through this experience, I began to realize that I was getting better. And God turned it all into good.

Just to wait and have patience is not hard if we become resigned to it, and do not despair. "Come unto me," says Jesus, "all ye that labour and are heavy laden, and I will give you rest. Take my yoke upon you, and learn of me; for I am meek and lowly in heart: and ye shall find rest unto your souls. For my yoke is easy, and my burden is light" (Matt. 11:28-30).

When you are uncertain as to what you should do in any given situation, it is always wise to just "wait on the Lord." Wait for His leading! Wait for Him to act! Wait as long as it is necessary to wait! Wait for Him to show you what to do!

If you are not sure of what you should or should not do, you may do the wrong thing. Pray for godly wisdom as you study God's Word and as you "wait on Him" to show you the way.

11. Depression as a Temptation

Previously I spoke of depression as a testing by God. Some there are who fail in the testing. They lose patience with God and turn to the world and sin, hoping that perhaps this will give them some release from their suffering with depression.

We sometimes see an acutely depressed, mentally ill person begin to show great boldness in worldly living as he never did before. His language may become foul, or he may take up smoking or drinking or both, over which he had previously gained victory, or he may become engaged in other questionable activities.

The reason for such changes is not a new love or craving for the things of the world. These things may even be less appealing than ever because of his illness. But a depressed person often does become confused, and the devil knows this and is ever ready to take advantage of this confused state. God's testing of His own is Satan's opportunity. He is ready to take advantage of the confused state of the depressed person and tries to beguile him into living for the world, telling him that it will free him from depression and bring him a measure of happiness which living for Jesus seemed to be failing to do.

I am reminded of how Satan tempted Eve in the Garden of Eden. At one point Satan said to Eve. "For God doth know that in the day ye eat thereof, then your eyes shall be opened, and ye shall be as God, knowing good and evil." We might paraphrase Satan's misleading counsel to Eve as follows: "You know what being good or obeying God is like, but you are only living a half life. You don't know what doing evil or disobeying God is like. If you eat this goodlooking fruit which appeals to your taste and appetite you will know what it is like to disobey God and to realize all the advantages that the eating of this fruit will give.

"You see, God does not want you to eat this fruit, because if you eat it you will become like God. But God does not want you to become like Him, because if you are like Him, He won't be able to boss you around any more.

"You do not know what you are missing. You need to 'live it up a little' so that you don't miss out on all the good pleasures of life."

Satan still tempts in the same way today, coming to the depressed with his lopsided argument which goes something like this: "By getting involved and enjoying the pleasures of this world, you will be able to forget your problems and not be depressed.

"Furthermore," argues Satan, "just take a look around you. Notice all the people who are much less concerned about righteous living than you are, and they are not suffering depression as you are. Just take a look! Could it be that you are hemming yourself in with a lot of pious rules and not allowing yourself enough freedom to enjoy worldly pleasures, and certain sins (although the devil doesn't call it sin) thereby bringing this depression upon yourself?"

Some psychiatrists and even pastors have been known to counsel those who come to them, to loosen up, live a little, and be more involved in the sins and pleasures of this world. Such counsel is never of God but always of the devil. I knew a sergeant in the army who encouraged his men, when depressed and discouraged, to get drunk or commit fornication because then they would be able to forget their troubles.

A question often asked and which is as old as sin itself is: "Just what is sin?" or, "What is not sin?" This has never been an easy question to answer, and Christians have often disagreed as to where to draw the line between sin and godliness or righteous living.

With some things we usually don't have a problem in knowing whether it is sin. It is very evident that it is sin. We know that murder and robbery are sins because the Bible clearly says they are. Even most non-Christians would not argue this. Many would also agree that adultery is a sin.

But there are things that would seem to be sin but the Bible does not come right out and say that they are sin.

The true Christian has another guide besides God's written Word to tell him what is sin and what is not. His first concern is to glorify Jesus. He will refrain from anything that would discredit Him or take attention away from Him.

Neither does he want, knowingly or unknowingly, to cause anyone to stumble into sin, because others might be looking to him as a role model.

It could be that some things which are a sin for some people may not be a sin for others because they are not tempted to do these things to excess or allow these things to lead them into deeper sin. Anything which would stand between us and our love for Jesus and become our first love is a sin.

However, the true Christian will guard his witness for Jesus. If a person allows himself to do many things which are questionable, some will doubt his Christianity, and rightly so. Besides being a stumbling block he will greatly limit the influence his testimony could have on the lives of others.

As we mature as Christians we will be better able to discern, or tell what is sin or a danger to our witness, and what is not. Some things which didn't seem to be sin when you first became a Christian might seem to be sin as you grow in grace and holiness and become more Christlike. The mature Christian also becomes more keenly aware of the seriousness of sin and of the enslaving hold it can have upon a person, and of how it can rob him of heaven. So he begins to hate sin like poison. He would rather refrain from doing something questionable than take a chance that if he became involved he might be sinning and be displeasing to God, and that it will damage his witness for Jesus.

I had quite a struggle with some thoughts regarding sin as a patient in a mental hospital, although no one pressured me to do what I had no freedom to do.

I was tempted, almost ready to try anything, even sin, if it would give me relief from my depression. But I did not yield. I was determined not to take any chances of disgracing my Lord. He was still my only hope. I would wait on Him and not take any chances by doing anything which I feared might make me displeasing to Him.

I was not sure if the things Satan tempted me with were sinful or not, but I wasn't going to take any chances. If I needed to make any changes in the habits of my life, I would wait until I was more stable emotionally and better able to think the whole matter through. I would not make any changes when I was not certain where those changes would take me, or what God thought about those changes.

These things had been settled earlier in my life, so when I got better I again saw all this more clearly. I did not believe God would be pleased if I made the changes. I was not tempted when I felt better, so I was kept from falling into certain sins.

Therefore, dear friend, when you are suffering from depression, beware of making any changes in habit which could be sinful or harmful to your soul. Do not let Satan deceive you with his illogical arguments. He is a very poor authority in telling anyone what to do when depressed.

Satan tempted Jesus when He was in the wilderness (Matt. 4:1-11). He will also tempt you and me when we are in a weakened condition. We need to be aware of his beguiling ways so as not to be led astray.

The question is sometimes asked, "Are there any worldly pleasures that are not sin?" At least there are things in this world that we can enjoy. We need to beware that we don't make everything to be sin. God has not said that everything of this world is sin or that we are not to have any pleasure or fun in this life.

I once had a Christian friend who very much limited himself in what he allowed himself to do. This impressed me and I thought that I should make him a role model for myself. I soon discovered, however, that I couldn't even cross the road without first asking myself if it was sin to do so. I was questioning every move I made and had little freedom to move. I then realized that this was silly and not right. We do have a conscience, and if we know our Bible we can trust our conscience and do what our conscience permits us to do. Nevertheless, we do need to be careful.

The Word of God must take precedence over the conscience which can be wrongly influenced by others, by the devil, or our old sinful nature and so lead us into sin. The Word of God will never do this to us.

The Christian has different motives and interests than what the people of the world have. We are a separated people with a special calling. Therefore, if something has become very popular with the people of the world, we should examine it very carefully in the light of God's Word and what our conscience would say to us before participating. We need to consider how it might affect our testimony or witness for Jesus.

There may be some things which would seem like sin to us, but we cannot label these things as sin or speak of them as such because the Bible does not make a clear declarative statement, calling these things sin.

But should our conscience speak to us about these things, we do well to listen and obey our conscience.

And how we live sometimes speaks louder than the words we speak.

12. Being Encouraged

Christianity is a warfare between good and evil. The Christian finds himself in the midst of this warfare and faces much pressure and stress from the evil forces as he takes sides with all that is good, righteous, or godly. When he finds himself in the midst of this warfare he often experiences discouragement, depression, and even defeat.

There are some things which the Christian can do, and should do to maintain his place in the battle. Even so, the enemy is real and the fight is intense. As he gives himself to this just cause he often becomes weary, tired, hungry and even sometimes spiritually wounded. To become acutely or clinically depressed is the same as becoming emotionally or spiritually wounded.

One of the best medicines for the Christian warrior is encouragement. Yet encouragement is not something which we can imagine we have or that we can work up in ourselves. It usually comes from a source outside ourselves.

We may often wish that we would receive more encouragement than we are getting as we attempt to glorify Jesus. We like to be assured that we are being appreciated when trying to do good.

Some people seem to get much praise and encouragement while others are starving for it. Encouragement is to the soul what food is to the body. It is what keeps us trying to do good. If we don't get much food, we try to make the little food we have go as far as we can. The same needs to be done when we receive only a little encouragement. We need to make the most of it and let it sustain us as much as we possibly can.

The Christian can find an ample supply of encouragement in God's Word, the Bible. But our soul also yearns for encouragement from others. The Bible tells us that we need to encourage each other.

Wherefore comfort yourselves together, and edify one another, even as also you do" (I Thess. 5:11).

Often a bit of encouragement comes our way and we don't even notice it or pay much attention to it. A mere "thank you" or positive comment from someone can be encouraging. We need to allow ourselves to be complimented, not just hear a good report and push it into the back of our mind and soon forget it. Rather, we need to think upon it, gather inspiration from it, and continue to do the good we are doing.

Sometimes Christians are reluctant to take compliments to heart for fear of becoming proud. But we can test ourselves to see if compliments make us proud or if they inspire us to do good.

If the compliment causes you to think only of yourself, or causes you to relax and come to a standstill in what you have excelled in, then it could be that selfish pride has taken over.

On the other hand, if you receive the compliment with a humble attitude and it encourages and inspires you to continue in the good you are doing, causing you to think of others and how you can be a help to them, and how you may bring glory to Christ by using the gifts and talents which He has given you; then you are truly receiving the compliment in a worthy manner and need to feast your soul on it.

We need encouragement in our fight against evil and sin. We encounter much that is discouraging. At times we may feel that no one notices the stand we are taking for Jesus and even cares less. It may seem, at times, that our Christian witness is falling on deaf ears.

If encouragement seems to be difficult to come by, we need to learn how we can let a little encouragement go a long way. I learned this lesson in the Veterans Hospital at Sturgis, South Dakota, back in 1964 when I was suffering from acute depression. (I tell in detail of this experience in my book, "My Experience with Clinical Depression," pages 97-101.) For a long time I seemed unable to find anything that encouraged me. Then one day just a bit of encouragement came my way. It was something which I could have easily overlooked, but I took encouragement from it. After that, I started looking for other bits of encouragement as a starving man will look for food. I was like a person who found a lost coin and began to look in the immediate area in hopes of finding more coins. I soon received other bits of encouragement and was again able to have some hope in what seemed like a hopeless situation.

However, there is a warning which needs to be heeded, as we begin to look for encouragement. Whatever we take encouragement in needs to be the truth, honest, just, pure and of good report. It needs to be virtuous and praiseworthy (Phil. 4:8). We must avoid being taken in by flattery and exaggeration. We should not think more highly of ourselves than we ought (Rom. 12:3).

But what is true about ourselves is worthy of our thought and food for encouragement, ever inspiring us by God's grace to continue to excel in the good we are capable of doing. Let us pray that we might be able to discern between truth and flattery.

It is very difficult to be encouraged when deeply depressed. If someone tells you that you seem better, you may imagine that this statement is only wishful thinking. You may imagine, and maybe even conclude, that this person is holding the real truth from you--and that you are a hopeless case.

But with Jesus all things are possible (Matt. 19:26). There is hope for you even though to you it may seem as if there is no hope.

There are many who have gone through the same valley of depression through which you are going. And they did "go through" the valley. They did not remain in it forever, as you might imagine for yourself.

Just remember, chances are that those who are trying to encourage you are not lying or flattering you but telling you the truth. Dare to believe them! When they say you are looking better, they know what they are talking about.

You may not be able to assure yourself of such hope, but you can prevent yourself from concluding that there is no hope--and this, you must do. Then, as stated above, with this optimistic frame of mind, look for signs of encouragement which will give you greater assurance that you are regaining and will regain your hralth. Do not give in to the temptation of thinking that all is hopeless, or interpret positive signs to be negative. Imagine the very best for yourself.

Be encouraged by the encouragement which others give you, and by the encouragement and promises of God which you find in God's Word, and in the way God has answered and is answering your prayers. Be encouraged by the way God blesses you from day to day. Don't allow those discouraging things to dominate your thinking. You can learn to control your thinking, at least somewhat, by dwelling on the bits of encouragement which have come your way.

If you have surrendered your life to Jesus for cleansing and re-shaping, try to see on the basis of God's Word how you qualify for God's eternal blessing which is heaven, and not His curse. Do not worry about what you can't do. God knows your limitations. He even knows how hard or impossible it is for you to pray and read your Bible while you are suffering from depression. If you can only pray short sentence prayers, then pray only short sentence prayers. If reading is difficult or even impossible at the present time, let the Holy Spirit help you to recall the Bible truths, (not necessarily by rote memory) that you learned earlier in life, and feed your soul on those truths. Remember that God has not changed, and He has not changed His attitude toward you.

As you seek this kind of encouragement, God, in due time, will give it to you as you continue to look to Him for it. But do not press or try to hurry God. He will give it in His time. Pray for patience and a willingness to wait on God for it. "Seek and you shall find" (Matt. 7:7). But God has not said how long we are to seek, and He does test our faithfulness (Gal. 6:9). Since He does try us, do not give up seeking. In the meantime, leave yourself open in letting God teach you and show you what His will is for you.

As you continue to seek these encouragements, be truly in earnest. God will not bless anything which we might attempt half-heartedly. Give it your best, and be as systematic as you can.

I found it helpful to write down in a notebook everything I found which was the least bit encouraging to me, giving the date when I first noticed or discovered it. You might find it best to do this at the end of each day. Let your mind think back over the day's activities and see if one or more things gave you at least a small measure of hope, happiness or encouragement; then record it. This will help you to remember these bits of encouragement when those things which discourage you seem to want to flood your thinking.

If you know what it is that is depressing you (sometimes we do not know what is depressing us or cannot put it into words), make this a matter of prayer. I suggest that you also write out your prayer requests in a notebook. Do not be afraid to ask the seemingly impossible of God (like healing you to get rid of your depression). But do not expect God to answer the request all at once, and don't tell Him how you want Him to do it. God, who is all wise, will do it in the best way for you and at the right time.

But you can look for signs that He is working at answering your prayers. For example: If your mate is not saved, dare to ask God to save his or her soul. Then, as you see signs of encouragement, like a bit of interest in the church, in God's Word, in other Christians, or in prayer or devotional reading, make a note of it. You may also wish to make note of new tenderness and love from your mate.

Keep adding to your list, recording all the encouraging things that occur no matter where the encouragement comes from or how insignificant it may seem at the time. You will be surprised at how much encouragement you will find to record as you seek for it.

From time to time, or when your depression crowds in on you, making you feel very discouraged, review the list of encouragements which you have recorded. Let them lift your spirit and assure you that God has not forgotten you.

Too often when we pray, we forget what it was we asked of God. If we do not remember what we asked of God we will not recognize God's answering our prayer request and forget to thank Him. We receive no encouragement from answered prayers, nor do answered prayer requests strengthen our faith as they should do.

If we write out our prayer requests in a note book, we do not need to make the same request over and over again. The Bible warns us that we shouldn't use vain repetitions when we pray (Matt. 6:7). The important thing is not that we keep hounding God with our prayer requests, but that we don't forget what it is that we asked of God. God does not forget.

After we have once made the request, we can leave it with God and just wait for Him to work it all out. In the meantime we are to remain in the spirit of prayer trusting God to work it all out for good. As time goes on we may wish to adjust our prayer request, which we should also record or adjust in our notebook.

Sometimes God says "no" to our requests. Paul after praying three times for healing, stopped praying for God's healing and was now ready to be content with His grace in being able to bear the suffering (II Cor. 12:7-8). God's answer to Paul was: "My grace is sufficient for thee" (II Cor. 2:9a).

If you are suffering from depression, let the encouragement you seek be in the areas that are related to your depression. You need not list things which you feel you should be thankful for but about which you feel no thanksgiving or from which you are receiving no encouragement. For example, you may feel you should be thankful for the food you have to eat, but you have no appetite. You can wait to list such things until you can again receive some enjoyment or satisfaction from them.

But do list everything that gives you even the least bit of encouragement, such as a compliment or "thank you" or a small favor from someone. Record whatever lifts your spirit at present. If in your deep depression you cannot think of anything to list, then ask God to give you something encouraging that will lift your spirit and wait on God for it. You may have to ask God to point it out to you, or help you to remember what you experienced which did lift your spirit. Look for a breakthrough in your depression. In my book, "My Experience with Clinical Depression," I describe this breakthrough as "The Golden Moment" (pages 97 to 101). It was something very small, only a feeling for a moment, but it did give me much encouragement in my depressed state as I kept thinking about it. It was a beginning. Soon other encouragements came.

Be encouraged in every way you can. If someone tells you that you are a good person, feel complimented, dwell on this all you can, and let it lift your spirit as high as it can. Let your imagination assist. Build a daydream around the compliment if you can. Let it push you up out of your depression as far as it will take you. Let it overshadow all the unpleasant thoughts which have haunted you. Among the benefits of such thinking is the keeping of depressing thoughts at bay. There is nothing which the depressed person needs quite as much as encouragement.

Let ne repeat: If you get only a little encouragement, let that little encouragement carry you a long way.

Encouragement is what Job very much needed, but his so-called friends, who visited him, only discouraged him and made him feel even more miserable. They tried to make him feel guilty, when conviction of sin was not his need. According to the Bible, Job was a godly man (Job 1:8), and his godliness was manifested in his life. These visitors should have reminded Job of how he had helped others and of the good he had done. They should have helped him to see the godliness that God had been able to weave into his character. This is what Job needed to be reminded of during his time of testing. He needed to be encouraged by having his self-esteem boosted.

This is what Christian friends are for. We need to encourage each other. To flatter or give an imaginary compliment of goodness or pious living is not of God. Our compliments must be truthful and honest as we attempt to be encouraging. One of the ways we can help a depressed Christian is to remind him of the Christian virtues which Jesus has been able to work into his life, and to help him to see the good he has been doing as a Christian.

Matthew 5:16 tells us to let our light shine in such a way that the world can see Jesus in our life and the Christian work we are doing. It is good for the depressed Christian to see this about himself. It will inspire him to press on in the good work he is capable of doing to the honor and glory of Christ.

We should love Jesus and live for Him. He who first loved us and did so very much for us should have priority or first place in our life. But we should let His love flow through us to those around us, especially to fellow Christians. We are to love and be considerate to those we come in contact with and be an encouragement to them. "As we have therefore, opportunity, let us do good unto all men, especially unto them who are of the household of faith" (Gal. 6:10).

The giving of compliments, which costs us nothing, is a very good way to give encouragement. It would be good if much more of this were being done. We need to look for good things in others, especially those close to us and other Christians we are acquainted with, letting them know that we notice and appreciate the good in them and the good they are doing. However, even as we should be careful that we are not taken in by flattery, we should also avoid flattery in complimenting others. Let what we say be truthful, honest, and without exaggeration.

It is wise and good to compliment children, especially our own children, giving them encouragement wherever we can. A compliment given in love often does more to gain obedience from our children than a direct command or scolding, although at times children also need to be disciplined.

Our immediate family is a good place to begin in giving compliments. We tend to take those close to us for granted, believing they already know how we feel about them, and to some extent we can take them for granted. However, it is good when members of a family voice their feelings for each other and give compliments.

Some claim that we need only to help the depressed to think positively and to change his pattern of thinking, and that will take care of his depression. Positive thinking is good, but before he can think positively he needs to be assured that he has something positive, something encouraging, to think upon which relates to what is causing him to be depressed. In other words, the circumstance which cause the depression must reveal some evidence of change for the better. The problem is not only in the mind of the depressed. It is circumstances which cause depression and should be made a matter of prayer. We must wait on God to make the changes in circumstances which are needed.

In other words, in order for positive thinking to take place, there must be a starting point, or a sign of hope for the depressed. There must be a sign from which the depressed can be encouraged and upon which he can build his hopes. The sign must be something more than just wishful thinking or an imaginative daydream. Philippians 4:8 states: "Finally, brethren, whatsoever things are true, whatsoever things are honest, whatsoever things are just, whatsoever things are pure, whatsoever things are lovely, whatsoever things are of good report, if there be any virtue, and if there be any praise, think on these things."

If the "whatsoever things" which give encouragement, are true, think on these things and let your mind dwell on them. When you hear honest, good, and true reports about yourself, for the sake of your own mental health you should think and meditate and let your mind dwell on such things, getting all the encouragement you can from such reports. Take them to heart and be lifted by them.

We do hear of how we need to be reminded of our sin, take conviction, and repent. Repentance, of course, is needful. But there is another side, especially when discouraged or depressed. We need to hear the positive about ourselves so that we can think positively about ourselves if we are Christian. After we admit and confess our sins to Jesus, we have every right to forget the sin of which we have repented. But the good we do should have a permanent place in our thinking and should always inspire us to do greater good, all to the glory of Christ.

There is much that would tend to defeat and discourage us in our attempt to fight the Christian warfare. Therefore, we need to take upon ourselves all the encouragement we can get in order to be inspired to continue on.

I told this to a depressed Christian woman once and she said, "Oh, but I never dared think too much about the compliments others gave me for fear of becoming proud." No wonder this woman was depressed. She thought only about that which brought her under conviction. I was able to help her to take encouragement, and it helped her to overcome some of her depression.

But we are not to be like the politician who thinks that after he has been elected, his goal has been reached and now he can live off the fat of the land. Wicked King Herod was like that. He thought only in terms of what he could get out of his kingdom and gave little thought towards serving the people. Rather, let us be like the politician who looked upon his office as an opportunity to do good.

When you are depressed it is hard for you to find enjoyment. Everything seems drab and depressing and does not appeal. It is needful that you seek some things which you can enjoy. This makes for a good healing from depression.

You may be a person who never sought enjoyment for yourself. Unselfishly you gave to others so they could enjoy life. This could vary all the way from letting someone else have the biggest piece of meat on the platter to a vacation by the lakeshore. Or you agreed to stay home and look after the business or farm while your partner went on vacation.

It is noble to think of others, but we all need some enjoyment. For the sake of our own mental health, we cannot afford to give others all of those things which would be an enjoyment to us.

I do not mean that we should selfishly get into an argument or fight over the biggest piece of meat. When we are Christians, some things lose their enjoyment if we have to fight or argue in order to get them. But many things can be obtained just by making our desires known. It is not a sin to enjoy life if done in a wholesome Christian way. Nor are we expected to give everything away which is rightfully ours and which can be to our enjoyment.

We may have had it drilled into us that it is more blessed to give than to receive. True it is more blessed to give but it is no sin to receive. If no one received, no one would have the joy of giving. We do well to have a spirit of giving and sharing, but we also need to learn to receive. We may need to be on the receiving end more at one time than at another. When we are sick or depressed, we do not need to feel guilty when we take from others what they freely give to us.

We do well not to be idle, but at the same time we should be careful not to be so occupied with a planned schedule that we miss little or big enjoyments that cross our path. Take time to appreciate the sunshine and flowers around you. Stop and visit a friend. Give a helping hand where you can. Be ready to become acquainted with a stranger or your next door neighbor, and always be ready to make a new friend. Take what enjoyment comes your way, but also seek for enjoyment. Some enjoyments or recreation may be too expensive, but do not feel that it is wrong for the sake of your mental health or need for a rest to spend some money on yourself. It is good stewardship and pleasing to God, and for health's sake, that you do this. Don't be afraid to try new things which are not sinful, in order to see if they might bring you a measure of enjoyment or satisfaction.

13. Encouragement Found in God's Word

The Word of God is meant to be a warning to the unsaved and an encouragement and guide to the Christian.

There are at least three outstanding, breathtaking encouragements which every dedicated Christian does well to take to heart in order to be inspired to carry on in the Christian warfare.

1. As a Christian we receive a new nature which does not sin and which is pleasing to God. "There is therefore now no condemnation to them which are in Christ Jesus, who walk not after the flesh, but after the spirit" (Rom. 8:1).

And because of this God looks upon us as His children and loves us more than any parent would love his or her children. "Behold, what manner of love the Father hath bestowed upon us, that we should be called the sons of God" (I John 3:1).

It is to such people that eternal life has been promised. "And if children, then heirs of God, and joint heirs with Christ" (Rom. 8:17). "Knowing that of the Lord ye shall receive the reward of the inheritance: for ye serve the Lord Christ" (Col. 3:24).

We hear and read little about the new nature of the Christian. It would be good to hear more. We do hear much more about the old nature. It seems to me that one of the keys to revival is to inspire the dedicated Christian with encouragement as he continues in his fight against temptation. For the child of God to realize that he has a new nature which is pleasing to God is certainly an encouragement to him.

However, even though as Christians we have a new nature, to our disappointment we also still have an old nature which can never please God. This is a real problem to the Christian. We wish we didn't have this sinful nature which we have to wrestle with constantly and keep under control in order that it does not dominate and ruin our life.

The old nature with its will to sin can be compared to weed seeds in the garden or grain field which tend to grow, crowd out and destroy the good plants. There are two ways to keep the weeds under control, and there are two ways to deal with our old nature. (a) We can make direct war on the weeds by digging them up or poisoning them. Likewise, we can make direct war on sin and our old Adam by exposing them as enemies of our soul and by repenting and refraining from continuing in those sins. And of course this needs to be done.

(b) Another way is to encourage the good seed to grow in our fields and crowd out the weed seeds by not giving them room to grow. Likewise, we can encourage the new life in Christ to grow and rule in our life and not allow the old Adam to influence and dominate our life. This second way is often the better, surer way.

2. The second great encouragement that God gives us in His Word is that if we confess our sins He will forgive them. "If we confess our sins, he is faithful and just to forgive us our sins, and to cleanse us from all unrighteousness" (I John 1:9).

As Christians, we do have an old Adam which keeps aggravating and tormenting us all the days of our life here on earth. But God gives us a weapon, a means whereby we can subdue this enemy of our soul. He offers forgiveness of all sins to all who repent. We need not let our sins stop or hinder us in our fight for righteousness.

This does not excuse us from straightening out what we have made crooked and can make right. It doesn't excuse us from righting the wrongs we can correct. But there is so much wrong in our lives, even as Christians, because we are careless, weak, or get carried away by the desires of the flesh, that we can never undo or make right again. To confess and admit such wrongs is all that God asks. He will blot such deeds from our record and they will never throughout all eternity ever be held against us. "He will turn again, he will have compassion upon us; he will subdue our iniquities: and thou wilt cast all their sins into the depths of the sea" (Micah 7:19).

But God not only forgives the wrongs we have confessed; He also does not remember them. "For I will forgive their iniquity, and I will remember their sin no more" (Jer. 31:34b).

If God will not remember our confessed sin, there is no reason that we should have to remember them. We, too, have every right to forget what has been confessed. However, the devil doesn't want us to forget. He often accuses us of what we as Christians have every right to forget, because he wants to discourage us. But thank God we do not need to listen to such accusations.

3. The third encouragement is that Jesus goes with us into the Christian warfare. He doesn't just put a burden on our hearts and turn us loose with a command to go forward. He goes with us, giving guidance, direction and help every step of the way. "Fear thou not; for I am with thee: be not dismayed; for I am thy God: I will strengthen thee; yea, I will help thee; yea, I will uphold thee with the right hand of my righteousness" (Isa. 41:10).

How good it is to know that we do not need to fight the Christian warfare alone or in our own strength. We may feel weak and most incapable at times, but even in our weakness Jesus promises to be our strength in our every need, giving us all that is needed to carry on. Nothing is expected of us in the way of service that our God doesn't provide so that we can do it. "Therefore I take pleasure in infirmities, in reproaches, in necessities, in persecution, in distresses for Christ's sake: for when I am weak, then am I strong" (II Cor. 12:10). "I can do all things through Christ which strengtheneth me.... But my God shall supply all your need according to his riches in glory by Christ Jesus" (Phil. 4:13, 19).

14. Being Idle

The definition of idleness is slothfulness or laziness, doing nothing, or doing nothing worthwhile. Idleness causes boredom. The devil tempts one to sin in order to escape boredom. Idleness may cause the mind to turn to thoughts of sex, filthy talk, self-pity, or petty grievances and offenses. Or idleness can cause one to be taken up with lying, gossip, revengeful thoughts and actions, or deeds of selfishness. Much evil can come from being idle (I Tim. 5:13).

Idleness also leads to useless worry. It is like a car spinning its wheels in the mud, working itself deeper into the mud and making no progress. It is the kind of worry that does not inspire action but finds an end in itself, its only purpose being to occupy an idle mind. Such useless worry can lead to depression and can aggravate depression (Matt. 6:31-34).

The worry caused by idleness causes one to panic, or to stagnate, rather than to seek a way out of the dilemma. Such worry is destructive to mental health. But worry, like stress, does have a healthful purpose in our lives. Instead of causing us to stagnate and relax, it should move us to action, to do what we can to eliminate the problem.

The opposite of being idle is being involved in doing something which has a useful or healthful purpose. Being involved not only includes work but also such things as good fellowship, clean play or recreation, hobbies, eating, sleeping, resting, or reading. We do well to remember that our time is not our own. As stewards of all that God has entrusted to us, we need to remember that our time, too, has been entrusted to us by God, and we are not to idle it away.

It is good for both physical and mental health to work or exercise so that we are tired and then to rest. We sleep better at night if we can go to bed with a tired body. The mind will relax better if the body is tired. If we spend the day in useful activity instead of worthless thoughts and useless worry, our minds will not as readily slip into what is harmful. We will go to sleep rather than lie awake, taken up with worry. We often hear, "Don't worry." However, we do not have it within us to stop worrying at will. If we do not give our minds something concrete and useful to think about, we will be filled with worry and can do little to stop it.

Sometimes older people, who eagerly look forward to retirement, slip into idleness when they retire. They are tired and long to rest. They vividly remember how good it was to have a day free from work and responsibility, so they think it wonderful if every day were like that. They dream that retirement will be that way, and they slip into idleness. Some people, who have worked hard at strenuous jobs all their lives and enjoyed their work, find upon getting older and weaker that they cannot do strenuous work any longer. Rather than look for easier work, they slip into idleness.

Yet idleness in older people causes the same bad effects as for anyone else. The shift to idleness brings with it boredom, a feeling of uselessness and depression. We are on this earth for a purpose until God calls us home. We do have to slow down when we get older, but it is dangerous to our mental health and state of happiness to drift into idleness. We do well to help our older people find new and useful interests which fit their limited strength and add meaning to their lives.

Now, if a person becomes more deeply depressed, it is harder to get him involved. One of the reasons for this is that the acutely depressed person temporarily loses some of his ability to concentrate. When this is the case, some kind of involvement which takes less concentration is needed. Sometimes there is a loss of interest in things that were once of great interest. The reason could be a loss of ability to concentrate which makes it difficult to get involved. Often acutely depressed people become idle and just sit. This, too, can be due to the inability to concentrate. They feel helpless to know what to do or how to spend their time.

We can help these people by getting them involved in something which takes less concentration. Involvement which fits the person's present ability and interest is always helpful for healing. In the acutely depressed, such involvement is not always easy to find, but an effort should be made. When I was suffering acute depression in the mental hospital, I had difficulty adjusting my activity until I found something that gave me inner satisfaction and a sense of accomplishment and was good for my mental health.

However, a loss of the ability to concentrate is not the only thing that hinders the depressed from getting involved. There is a feeling of listlessness and lack of ambition which weighs him down. There is a temptation just to remain idle, or a dislike for any kind of activity. Some efforts need to be made to fight this feeling and to get involved, even if one does not feel like getting involved. Self-exertion and willpower need to be exercised.

When the depressed, in their temptation to remain idle, are reminded of the unpleasant fruits of idleness and experience boredom, uncontrolled worry and depression, they are more ready to fight their listless feelings and their temptation to be idle and will get involved.

We should not be idle. Idleness is damaging to our mental health; it is closely related to procrastination. We need a purpose in life in order to see some worth in ourselves.

When we become physically idle, our minds do not stop thinking. It is like a car shifted into neutral and just idling. It is still running but it isn't pulling any load or going anywhere. The idle mind has to find something to occupy itself. If it can't be taken up with planning and carrying out work or some worthwhile life plan, it is apt to be taken up in needless worry or something worse. Idleness leads to boredom, which can lead to sin for the lack of excitement.

The mind tires even as the body tires. The mind also tires when idling, as described above. And if the mind works, using its energy in useless thinking, while the body is idle, the mind will tire while the body is still full of unspent energy. This can cause a feeling of fatigue when the body is not fatigued. It may cause a tired feeling and sleeplessness. It is good when the mind and body can tire together and rest together, which is conducive to both mental and physical health.

It is needful that we be occupied with worthwhile activity. We are not to waste our time; we will be held accountable to God for how we spend it. We need to find a balance between idleness and being too busy and under constant pressure.

15. Daydreaming

Daydreaming, if it is good daydreaming (not taken up with useless worry or lustful thinking) is good for our mental health and is closely related to getting involved. Often, it precedes getting involved.

Healthy daydreaming is not just fanciful and wishful thinking. Good daydreaming is imagining yourself to be doing thrilling things and accomplishing good within the realm of your present ability to achieve. We have many more daydreams than we can ever hope to realize. Both time and circumstances prevent this. But it is relaxing and also challenging to the mind to think about these things. We can gain joy and satisfaction in thinking through and planning events in our minds just as if we were actually going to do them. There are many things in life, both good and bad, which we read, hear and experience, which inspire and direct our daydreaming.

For example, you may see some social evil in our land and long to do something about it. You imagine in your mind just what kind of laws you would put into effect if you had the political power and influence to do so. If your desire is strong enough to make this dream a reality, you might enter politics and seek the office that would give you power to make the dream a reality, or join some group working toward that end. Or it may all end just as a dream. Some dreams might involve a lifetime ambition or many years to realize fulfillment, like the one mentioned above. Other dreams can be dreamed and realized in a short time and would demand much less involvement to be fulfilled. But every good dream is good for mental health and serves a purpose even if it is never fulfilled.

But the acutely depressed, may find

it difficult to daydream. I found it difficult and even impossible when suffering from acute depression. All my dreams ran into some problem or reminded me of some worry which was depressing to me. And I was not able to control this worry. I felt I had sunk so low that I could not enjoy anything, even a good daydream. How thankful I am now that I can again daydream!

The loss of concentration, which sometimes accompanies acute depression, affects one's ability to daydream. An understanding friend can be helpful to a depressed person. As they together try to imagine and plan a meaningful future for the depressed person, the friend can make helpful suggestions for solving some of the problems and fears he keeps bumping into. His friend can mention some appealing activity which the depressed can think on.

We do well to encourage the depressed to daydream and to make some plans for the future, helping him to see that some of the things which seem impossible may not be as impossible as he thinks, and that all things are possible through Christ.

Daydreaming is good for our emotional makeup and should never be classified as idleness. Often our minds can be occupied with healthy daydreams while we do routine work. This is helpful to mental health in alleviating the boredom of routine labor.

Daydreaming often opens the way for us to become involved in some particular way. The reverse is also true. When we let our minds and bodies become involved with purposeful activity our minds will more readily shift to daydreaming for a change of pace, rather than to useless worry.

We do well to let our minds daydream. However, we should not be content with just daydreams. This can be harmful to mental health and stability. An effort should be made to fulfill some of our dreams; many ambitions find their roots in daydreams.

After deciding that we want to make the daydream a reality comes careful planning. This, too, is challenging and good for the mind, to look ahead and figure out in some detail how to do those things we have set our hearts and minds on doing.

16. Work

It is good to plan our day, to figure out what is most important. It may be wise to do the most important tasks first. Do not leave the most unpleasant task until last if at all possible. Also, plan for some pleasure, and then follow the plan.

Do not be so rigid in planning that you cannot allow for needed adjustment and unexpected interruptions. We should not race with ourselves, always trying to set new records. Medical experts tell us that this can lead to an early heart attack.

It is well to plan our work well enough to be organized and orderly yet not under undue pressure. Pressure is not good for mental health. We cannot always avoid it, but careful planning will do much to eliminate it. For mental health's sake, it is good to take one thing at a time, in orderly fashion, and enjoy doing it.

In order to avoid monotony and boredom, it may be wise to have several well organized jobs going at the same time, and then change off, working first on one and then on another. But beware of starting more things than can be finished.

Personally, I find it helpful to do the unpleasant and harder things in the forenoon or early part of the day, saving the pleasant and more relaxing jobs for late afternoon or evening. At times, when faced with something more challenging or unpleasant late in the day, I will put it off until the next forenoon, or for some forenoon when I am free to work on it.

I try not to let new challenges interfere too much with what I am presently involved with. This does away with confusion. When I lay aside or quit a certain task, it helps to stop at a convenient place. This makes it easier to go back to it at a later time, and it takes less time to figure out again how to go ahead. I find this helpful especially in my writing.

As a pastor, with studying, writing letters and other desk work ever before me, I find it best if I classify this work as my hardest (because it takes the most concentration) and do it early in the day. Garden work, washing the car, and chores around the house are more relaxing. I find that if I put these other things first during the day, it is much harder to get into the mood for doing the work at my desk. I can enjoy desk work more if I do it first.

As I said, some worries are good. And it is good when such concerns inspire us to look ahead and plan well the steps that need to be taken to alleviate the worry. Our planning should take into account the things that worry or concern us, to see what we can do about these things and when would be the best time to do it. Take one thing at a time, think it through, see what can be done, and find a place for it in your well-planned schedule.

We have a tendency to push unpleasant things out of our minds. We say to ourselves, "I just am not going to let it worry me." But we need to let it worry us into action. If we say we are not going to worry about it, we only push it into our subconscious where it lies and festers, only to haunt us again and again in the future, or at night in nightmares, to the detriment of our mental health. It is much better for mental health to face the problem, pay the price, and do what must be done so that we can free our minds from any more thought over the matter.

It is good to have a work plan as we begin our day and then to follow that plan, as long as it is not so rigid that it won't accommodate little emergencies or whatever demands your attention on the spur of the moment. It should not be so rigid that you can't enjoy God's gifts of sunshine and flowers to brighten your day, or take time for a bit of fellowship with a neighbor or a friend or a stranger who happens to cross your path. Beware not to set your goals too high for a given day. It is good for mental health to plan for some fun or wholesome recreation.

And it is most important to plan to take time to sit at Jesus' feet and learn of Him--in other words, to read and study our Bibles. We need to use some of our time to listen to what God has to say to us. And, as we read and study God's Word, we need also take time to meditate on that Word and to pray. It is important that we take time for the care of our soul needs as well as our bodily needs. Too often, no such plans are made, time slips away, and our soul is neglected. A study of God's Word will also help us know how best to plan and spend our time.

17. Procrastination

Now let me say a word about procrastination and how this can be a hindrance to good mental health. Everything which we have in our minds to do, both big and little tasks, pleasant and unpleasant, and especially those things which we ought to do or must do, are like weights until we get them done to our satisfaction. Then we can dismiss them and no longer feel their weight. To put off such tasks, or to push them into the subconscious for the present, does not help. It only shifts the weight so we do not feel it quite so much at the time.

Now if we have many unfinished tasks on our minds, or let them pile up, or if some tasks which could and should have been done earlier suddenly become urgent, we feel under pressure and imprisoned by our work. This pressure tires the mind and can bring on a feeling of depression.

Then, if some storm or stress situation comes into our lives at the same time, we will be much less capable of handling it because we already are enslaved to a multitude of unfinished tasks which brings weight on our minds. The weight of the stress will be much heavier because of all the other things already weighing us down. Continually living in this kind of situation is damaging to mental health. If the situation is acute enough and the weight heavy enough, it could cause a mental breakdown with acute depression.

Those little tasks which have a tendency to pile up and weigh us down can vary all the way from taking out the garbage to repairing the leak in the roof. The sooner we complete such tasks, the sooner we are able to ease our minds from their weight.

If we have some major work project

coming up, or something else which will take our all and our best, including full concentration, it is good first to clear the board by completing little, unfinished tasks so that we do not feel their weight while giving our best to the major project. This will help us do our best.

We talk about overwork causing a heart attack, but within the mind of the one who overworks is a long list of unfinished work which is pressuring and enslaving him, driving him to work beyond his capacity. The root of the problem is not overwork but taking on too much work.

Some people seem to be able to live and work under the pressure of a heavy work load. However, to carry a constant overload of unfinished work in the back of our minds does nothing for our mental health and can be a form of slavery. Some people claim they can work better under pressure, but it is a known fact that any kind of pressure over a long period of time can be damaging to health. It is rather sad, I fear, when we have to rely on pressure to inspire us to get going. What is apt to happen when we get into the habit of relying on pressure to motivate us is that when not pressured we become so relaxed (consciously or unconsciously) as not to want to think about the work that demands our attention. We become like the horse who is constantly being whipped in order to get him to go. The horse becomes so dependent upon the whipping that he doesn't go unless whipped. We can become so dependent on pressure to get us to work (all out of habit) that we have difficulty making ourselves work when we are not under pressure.

We never know when we will have to face some crisis situation. If at such a time we are free from the pressure of other immediate responsibilities we could have taken care of earlier, we will be better able to cope with the crisis situation and will not have the burden of an added heavy load.

Now I should like to say a word to pastors as they face the many tasks of serving a parish. What I said previously about planning our day and doing the important and harder things early in the day can also apply to a week's activity. It is important that a pastor carefully plan his week, because his work divides itself into weeks.

The most important task the pastor faces every week is preparing his sermon. It is wise, and much better for mental health, to prepare the sermon early in the week, even on Monday or Tuesday, and not let the thought of this task haunt one all week long. I discovered that when I prepared the message for Sunday morning early in the week, with all the time I needed available and without the pressure of a deadline as would be the case if I waited until Saturday, then I could enjoy preparing that message much more and I prepared a better message.

Some pastors say they can do better work under pressure. I do not argue this point, but it does not fit me. However, whether or not they do better work under pressure, pressure is not good for the mental health. Over a long period of time it can also be damaging to the heart.

As pastors, we can put the Holy Spirit under pressure in enlightening us on a text we are to preach by not giving Him time to teach us. This can cause our sermons to be shallow, unenlightening, and unchallenging. I am convinced that when preparing a sermon we need a quiet time, free from cares that demand our immediate attention and long enough for the Holy Spirit properly to teach and inspire us. Surely, early in the week, when we are not surrounded by weekend pressures, is a better time than later in the week.

18. Too Much Ambition

Now let us consider the opposite extreme of being idle, and see what effect being over-ambitious, has on our mental health. In the Bible we have the example of Martha (Luke 10:38-42), who let herself become frustrated by a multitude of household duties.

The problem is not in doing too much work but in taking on too much responsibility. Work done is always a relief to the mind; once it is done you can forget about it. But when we take on more work than we have time to do, the mental load of unfinished tasks does not get lighter and we cannot find time for adequate rest. It is like pumping water out of a swamp: the water fills in as fast as you pump it out.

This was Martha's problem. Perhaps she should have planned her work better and had all these unfinished household duties done before Jesus arrived. Or maybe she felt that it all had to be done right away, yet the work she was doing was not that urgent. Jesus indicated that she should have scheduled her time in a way that she could take advantage of His being there and learning from Him. Martha's problem, I believe, was more in poor planning, or in taking on too much responsibility, than in overwork. We do learn from Scripture that there is a time to work and a time not to work. Sunday, for example, is a time not to work (especially at some things) but that time should be spent sitting at Jesus' feet and learning from Him. If we take on too much work, or have many unfinished tasks on our minds that could have been done earlier, it will be harder for us to relax on the Lord's Day and give our full attention to Him.

19. Fear

The Bible tells us not to fear (Luke 12:32). Some interpret this admonition to mean that it is a sin to fear and that God is giving us a stern command not to fear, or else! I do not believe that God's command has been given with quite this strong an overtone. If I had to think of fear as a sin which I had better not commit, I would feel guilty every time I was afraid.

When Jesus tells us not to fear, I believe He is speaking in a gentle tone and is not so much saying, "You must not fear," as, "You need not fear." And then He tells us why we need not fear: because He is always with us (Heb. 13:5) and will never leave nor forsake us. He says, "Fear not," for our comfort and encouragement rather than to admonish us.

Certain fears are damaging to an individual's capacity to function normally and enjoy life in a full way. These can be very enslaving. We should try to conquer them so they do not conquer us. Jesus will help us to conquer them. These fears can weigh on our minds just as unfinished tasks do.

Before we go any further in this line of thought, we need to recognize that there are some things we need to fear and should fear, like getting too close to a burning building or daring to sin. The first thing we need to do is to separate those things we always need to fear from those fears we should conquer. There are a number of things mentioned in the Bible that we should fear.

There seems to be a curve relating to the fears in our lives we need to conquer. We come into this world with a lot of fear. One of the greatest needs of a newborn baby is to learn to feel secure and not be afraid.

Therefore, a baby needs much love and cuddling. Little children often fear being too far away from their mothers. They both anticipate and fear the first day of school. As they grow older, they learn to conquer these fears, one by one.

It seems that in the late teens we have the fewest fears. At that time we feel we can conquer the world. Sometimes at this age we are not able to distinguish well between those fears we should respect and those we should conquer. This is especially true of boys who can become very daring and take foolish chances. This is why car insurance rates are much higher for teenage boys and young men. Alcohol consumption also can cause one to throw caution to the wind and try to conquer all fears, even those we should not conquer. Then, as we get older, we again tend to become over-cautious and take on needless fears.

Proverbs 22:13 states, "The slothful man saith, There is a lion without, I shall be slain in the street." There are two things we should notice here in relation to fears we should try to conquer. First, there really is not a lion in the street, and it is foolish to have such a fear or excuse for not going into the street. If the man who fears the lion would muster up enough courage just to step outside his house, he would see that there is no lion there and his fear of going out would vanish. How foolish to imagine fears where there are none! We do well to investigate imaginary fears so as not to let them drive us into a corner or cause us forever to remain indoors. We need to overcome such fears so that we can dare to venture out, enrich and broaden our lives, and find many more enjoyable things to do.

Second, we notice that it is the slothful or idle person who is likely to become enslaved with needless fears. Idleness breeds fear. Rather than remain idle we need to set out and conquer needless fears.

Now let us look at some examples. Some people, often older people, are afraid to ride in airplanes. Now, in order to live life to the fullest it is not necessary to learn to ride in an airplane without fear. But the risk to airplane passengers is actually lower than to automobile passengers. Thus it is really foolish to fear an airplane ride. If the person who has this fear would take courage and try just one airplane trip, he would soon realize how little risk there is and how comfortable air travel can be. He would be able to conquer his fear. Many who once feared the plane ride have overcome their fear and now experience plane travel as a thrilling pleasure.

Having conquered one needless fear, we find it easier to conquer others. Conquering fear is like conquering new territory. The greater the beachhead, the easier it is to advance.

Another useless fear is that of speaking before a group of people. Once you have done it, your fear diminishes and you begin to find pleasure and satisfaction in public speaking.

As we become adults, we learn to overcome needless fears one by one. Each year of growth brings new fears we need to conquer. I remember how as a teen-ager I feared asking a girl for a date lest she would refuse. It took me a long time to overcome this fear. But when I gained courage to venture out, I learned two things: That sometimes girls say "Yes," and that a "No" was not impossible to live with.

If we have had to curtail some activity for a while, like not driving a car during a prolonged illness, or after an accident, we may have developed some fears in starting to drive again and will have to regain the confidence we once had. Older people often experience such fears. They know they cannot act as quickly or as proficiently as they once did, and they become disappointed in themselves. They may give up altogether for fear of disappointing themselves.

We must learn to expect less from ourselves as we grow older. If we expect less, we are less likely to give up and quit. We need to be ready to face new challenges and cope with needless fears that would tend to inactivate us before our time. To allow our lives to become overrun with needless fears is damaging to our mental health.

We may not always be able to prevent fear from invading our lives. It may come with periods of sickness or depression or just because we are getting older. But we do best not to hide behind such fears, ever reluctant to venture out again, lest fear rob us of joy and satisfaction in life. With God's help we can dare to face needless fears one by one. As we do, they will disappear.

Even though we grow old, we need to work at staying young as long as we can. God wills that we use what He has given us as long as we are able. We are of no help to ourselves or others if we let ourselves wither away before our time on earth is finished. We do well to remain active. This is good stewardship of our time and of all that God has entrusted to us.

We should also seek to expand our lives even though we are deteriorating and growing older. We can do this by daring to venture out and by conquering needless fears. We must not let the lion which is not in the street keep us indoors!

We often hesitate in trying new things, or trying to achieve in a new area of our lives, for fear of failing. We need to realize, as Christians, that God works all things out for our good (Rom. 8:28), even our failures, and that failure builds character, often more than success does. To fail is not the end of the world, and success often is built on a number of failures. Failure may lead to success eventually while idleness, or refusing to try, will never gain anything for us.

We can be of help to others if we can assist them to sort out their fears and then to face and conquer them. People who are undergoing depression have many fears which often completely hem them in. We can help them by encouraging them to conquer their fears one by one, thus relieving their depression.

I had many fears to conquer as I recovered from acute depression. I feared being with my own family again. I feared preparing sermons again and, even more, preaching them. I feared failing and having to face the fact that I could not preach. This was a needless fear. By trying I discovered that I could preach, and I was greatly encouraged. I feared driving a car. I feared facing a new day. All of these areas had to be conquered.

We might ask where needless fears come from. They come because of ignorance, an ignorance we cannot help because we are born in ignorance. It is these fears that we can and should overcome by learning so that we do not have to be enslaved by them.

What, then, are some of the things we should fear? We are to fear God, which means that we should not only have a desire to please Him but also exercise care so as not to displease Him.

We should have a fear of the devil and watch out for his subtle lies and tempting ways.

We need to have a fear of love for the world and our old sinful nature, so as not to allow them to lead us astray.

And we are to fear that which would endanger our body and soul. To fear is to be cautious.

20. Worry

It is easy to say to someone, "Don't worry," or, "It is foolish to worry." In time, to be continually worried about something will bring on depression. But as was said before, we cannot just shut off our minds from worrying as we would shut off a water spigot. It is likely that if we have something to worry about, we will spend a lot of time worrying even if we prefer to forget it.

We may not be able to stop worrying but we can do something about not having so much to worry about. We can lessen our minds' load by carefully planning and by not taking unnecessary chances. We can plan and live our lives in such a way as to prevent worry. It is how we live, rather than the will of the mind, which will prevent us from worrying.

As was mentioned, it is well to flee idleness, face needless fears, take encouragement, not live in sin, and, most important of all, wait on God, pray aright, and read our Bibles for edification. We should take comfort and encouragement wherever and whenever we can, especially from God's Word.

But let me mention something else. How we manage our finances can do much to prevent worry. It is easy to tell someone who fears his money will not reach, "Don't worry, God will take care of you." And it is true that God will take care of His own. Yet we do not have the liberty to expect God to take care of us if we carelessly spend the money we earn, money He has entrusted to us. To buy on credit and continually have to pay a high rate of interest and make monthly payments can get very wearisome. Also, it is enslaving. The Bible tells us that we should not willfully enslave ourselves to others (I Cor. 7:23).

It is a wonderful feeling to be debt free. This feeling goes much further toward a life of contentment and peace than having a lot of comforts that bring pleasure but are not paid for. We also do well when we plan and save for a "rainy day."

Many people say that they live only once. They say: "We are young only once; if we are not able to get and enjoy certain temporal things now which will give us pleasure, we will be too old to enjoy them when we can afford them." Since they feel they will never be able to afford to pay cash for them, they buy on credit, and they pay dearly later on.

But let us remember that as Christians we are not on this earth, first of all, to enjoy life, but to prepare for eternal life and to serve Christ. We need not envy those who have more of this world's goods than we do. If we have Christ, and thus have treasure and an inheritance in heaven, we are much better off than those who do not know Christ, no matter how much temporal wealth they may have.

We do well to live within our means, manage our money well, live free of debt as far as possible, and make our desires known to Christ. If it is good that you have such desires He will help you to get the thing you desire and get it when it is best for you to have it. The best way to prevent financial worry is not to have needless financial obligations to worry about.

What is true about our finances is also true of the body. We are to watch over it and take care of it because it is the temple of God. We should not put into the body anything that will harm it, such as tobacco, alcohol or other harmful drugs. The right diet, good eating habits, exercise and proper rest are a few practices we can follow in order to maintain good health.

Yet no matter how well we take care of our bodies, we are not guaranteed perfect health. Some people are born sick or crippled; others are afflicted later in life; we can do little to prevent this. Also, no matter how careful we are, accidents will occur. But we can help the situation by not adding to it, or making it worse by our own carelessness. It is our carelessness in these matters which gives us cause to worry. We need not worry about what we cannot help; we can accept it as God's will for us, knowing that He will work it out for good.

God has given us consciences, and our consciences can do much to prevent us from being taken up with undue worry. We should never go against conscience or better judgment. To do so can cause much anxiety. It is not possible to go against one's conscience and be free of worry thereafter.

If you do not obey conscience, you will have no end of worry, and there will be little you can do to stop worrying. Whenever you are facing a major decision in life or are tempted to do something you feel hesitant about, please do not rush into it. Take time to pray about it at length and to think it through carefully, both pro and con. Ask God for wisdom to make a wise decision. He promises to give wisdom to those who ask Him for it (Jas. 1:5). Give Him time to reveal His will in the matter before deciding. Remember, it is better not to act than to regret having done it.

On the other hand, if you get a signal to go ahead, you should not hesitate to step out. There is also a danger in being overly cautious. To have had an opportunity and then failed to act on it can bring regret. Again, ask God for wisdom and act on that wisdom. Do not decide hurriedly if not under pressure to make a quick decision.

21. Prayer and Bible Study

Prayer is talking to God. His Word, the Bible, is God's first and most common way of speaking to us. God also speaks to us through experience but never in a way contrary to the teachings of His Word. Our experience, when seen in the light of God's Word, will verify the truth of Scripture and strengthen our faith in it.

Because the Bible is God's first and most common way of speaking to us, prayer and the reading and studying of God's Word should always go together. They are the ingredients necessary to make conversation or a meaningful relationship between God and man. When one of these elements is missing, the relationship is not complete, and misunderstanding can develop between God and man as to what is truth.

It is dangerous to pray and not read the Bible. We live in an age when there is much stress on prayer but not the same emphasis on reading and studying God's Word. This reveals a selfishness in man, in which he wants much from God but is not willing to be led by God or accept responsibility from Him.

Several decades ago the opposite was the trend. Stress was put on the study of Scripture, but it was not always done with a humble attitude. Prayer and reading of Scripture in a prayerful attitude, looking to the Holy Spirit for interpretation and teaching, was not stressed. The result was that people began to question Scripture and to doubt that it was inspired by God. Liberal theology with a belief in evolution was the result. We must keep a balance between prayer and study of Scripture; we should not engage in one to the neglect of the other.

Prayer is more than just asking God

for what we want. God is not a Santa Claus to whom we can write letters in the form of prayers, asking that our "stockings" be filled with what we desire. Prayer is doing business with God. He has a work for each of us to do. Our main purpose in prayer as Christians, once our sins are forgiven, is to gain guidance and leading from God as to what He expects of us. The requests we make of Him are to be like requisitions, asking for what is needed directly or indirectly so that we can do what He wants us to do.

Self-dedication is an important factor in an effective prayer life. I shall never forget when I was seriously sick with a rather prolonged illness as a boy. I told God that if He made me well, I would serve Him in whatever way I could be of greatest service to Him. I regained my health much more quickly than my doctor had expected. I always felt that my dedication had much to do with this quick healing. God has never allowed me to forget that promise and I remain dedicated to do His will.

Neither is prayer a key to a carefree, successful life. Since its purpose is to gain guidance in doing God's will, it is apt to lead us into involvement and trying situations that accompany that warfare. Prayer will help us to face and overcome such difficulties, but it is no assurance that we will escape them. A prayerful, dedicated life might even lead us into a spiritual desert area where we see little spiritual life or repentance of sin. But thanks be to God, we will not be counted worthy according to the fruits we produce but according to our faithfulness in witnessing. "Moreover it is required in stewards, that a man be found faithful" (I Cor. 4:2).

Much stress is put upon the quantity

of prayer but little is said about the quality of prayer. Yet it is quality rather than quantity which counts with God. James 5:16b tells us: "The effectual fervent prayer of a righteous man availeth much." It is not hard to realize that it is the mature Christian (the righteous man) who has advanced the farthest in the school of prayer. It is not the many words but a heart in tune with God's heart, acquainted with His will and purpose and dedicated to it, that avails much. A mature Christian best knows how God wills he should pray and what requests to make in doing business with God according to His terms.

God is not pleased with endless, vain repetition (Matt. 6:7). We are not to try to wear God down with requests to which He has said "No," or which He hesitates to grant. We can pray such requests and then leave them with God. We need not continuously hound Him for them.

Scripture tells us that Paul prayed three times for healing (II Cor. 12:8). It does not say he prayed four, five or more times for healing but only three times. After the third time he stopped asking God for it and accepted the fact that his "thorn" was God's will. Instead, he was to receive the grace to bear it.

Too often when we pray we shift into a prayer mood, giving thanks and making requests for whatever comes into our minds. After we have finished praying, we may not be able to recall what it was we prayed for. We know that God hears and remembers, but it is important that we remember also. If we do not remember what we pray for, we will not realize it when God answers our prayer but will attribute the answers to natural causes. And to have God fulfill our prayer request when we cannot remember what we requested will do nothing toward strengthening our faith.

Again, as mentioned previously, I find it helpful to write my requests in a notebook and occasionally to check this list to see to what extent God has honored my request. I discover that often He has not fully granted my request but is in the process of granting it. He, in His good time, is working it out. Sometimes He says "No." In some instances, as time goes on, I feel led to withdraw or adjust my request. Either the situation relating to the request has changed, or I have been led to see that I prayed amiss: what I asked was not altogether according to God's will.

Prayer is not so much a time when we verbally talk to God, although there is a place for that, but more often just being close to God as we walk continuously in the spirit of prayer. We can think our prayers as well as say them, since God knows our thoughts even before we think them (Ps. 139:2). We can think with God, letting Him put thoughts into our minds (never contrary to His Word), as we face the various responsibilities He places upon us.

Again, the important thing is not how long we pray, but that we thoroughly think through with God all the business we have with Him. What has been settled with God and oneself can be left with God. It does not need to be repeated over and over again.

We sometimes feel that the reason we have not received quicker results to our prayer requests is that we have not prayed loud enough or often enough. But loud talk and persistent pleading are not what God desires of us. We can be wearing on God, as children sometimes wear on their parents for something the parents hesitate to give. Sometimes, when this happens, parents hesitantly give in against their own better judgment, to the regret of all concerned later on. God, too, may go against His better judgment and give us what we ask, if we are overly insistent, but this is never to our good. The children of Israel prayed that God would give them a king. This request was not pleasing to God, but because of their insistence God granted the request nevertheless. Over a long period of time it led to the spiritual downfall of God's people.

We must learn to wait on God. We like to feel, as Christians, that prayer gives us a key to all of God's power and resources, such as the power to heal, peace within ourselves, and other material and spiritual needs as well as certain desirable pleasures. And though this statement may be true in a very limited degree (prayer does change things), in a broader sense it is not true. God does not trust any of us to that extent. He has not given us, even through prayer, access to all of His vast resources. We do not have the freedom to help ourselves to them at will. Sometimes God says, "No" or "Not yet."

We can freely ask at any time. God does not begrudge our asking, but we do not always receive. We receive only when it is according to His will. God is not a jack-in-the-box who jumps when we push the button.

Some people, in their zeal to minister and be a spiritual help to others, act as if they have a corner on God and that He especially favors their requests. God is not a respecter of persons in this way. He may more readily hear the mature Christian (the righteous man, Jas. 5:16b), but this is because the mature Christian has learned to pray according to God's will. In Old Testament times the people needed to approach God through another, a priest, but such a mediator is no longer needed. Everyone can freely go to God with prayer requests, and if a request is in line with God's will, He will hear it just as readily from us as from anyone else. He will also hear when we pray for physical healing.

When we pray for others we do well to remind them in some way that we cannot hurry God. We must be patient and wait on Him. In the meantime, we can be sure that God is well aware of all our hurts and needs, as well as the hurts and needs of those we pray for, and that He will not forget us.

Jesus, who drank the cup of suffering to the last drop, knows all about it. He gives as requested, or He gives grace to endure. Our place is to trust Him and be patient. When Jesus heard that Lazarus, whom He loved dearly, was seriously ill, He waited two days before going to Bethany. And when He arrived, according to man's reasoning, He was four days too late--Lazarus had been dead that long. But Jesus was not too late, and He acted according to God's timing and worked all things out for good (John 11).

You see, God has a purpose for all suffering, including depression. He has promised to work it out for good (Rom 8:28). We have to give God a chance so that this good can be realized. If He granted our requests the minute we asked them, we would miss much of the blessing He wants us to gain through the problems we face.

When I was sick in the mental hospital, a healing service was held for me but no instant healing was realized. If God had granted our request for healing immediately, I would not have learned all that God wanted me to learn through this experience. The blessing was worth the waiting.

We should have a system in our Bible study so that as we continue on, day after day, year after year throughout our lives, we eventually will have at least a general idea of what the Bible says as a whole. Matthew 4:4 says: "Man shall not live by bread alone, but by every word that proceedeth out of the mouth of God." We see the emphasis on the little word "every" here. No part of the Bible should be overlooked in our attempt to know God's truth.

A good way to study the Bible is as a book. You may start at the beginning of the Bible with Genesis (the beginning of a book is always a good place to begin), or the beginning of the New Testament with Matthew, or you may study some other book of the Bible from beginning to end. As you study, try to find the general theme or main emphasis of that book. Thereafter, when a certain verse is given and interpreted from that book, you can see if the interpretation parallels the main thought of the book. If there should be a genealogy which bogs you down in your study, skip over it and go on.

The tendency for many today in reading the Bible is to read it in a hit-and-miss fashion. They read a little here and a little there, then sort of piece it together, making the Bible say what they want it to say. Or they read it in a topical way, trying to pick out what the Bible says on a certain subject, or just what is especially interesting to them at the time. They treat the Bible like a catalog or reference book, reading only small portions, and they neglect reading large parts of it. They have no system in their Bible reading. But the Bible was not written that way. Originally it was not even divided into chapters and verses. It seems very unlike an orderly God to scatter what He wants us to know throughout the Bible, making us hunt for what is important (or important to us). He wants us to know the whole truth from the whole Bible.

The danger of this hit-and-miss system is that we read the Bible out of context and fail to see how what we read relates to the truth or the whole Bible. In many cases, when the Bible is read in this way, the wrong interpretation is given and it does not agree with the truth of the rest of the Bible.

It is a mystery to many why there are so many differences of opinion. The problem is not in what the Bible says, but in the various ways in which it is studied. Too many people make one verse, a few verses, or a portion of Scripture their whole Bible. They emphatically cling to the exact wording of these portions, believing each word to mean what they think it means (words do vary in meaning). They pay no heed to what the rest of the Bible might have to say about that same doctrine. If everyone were more concerned about living from every word which the Bible says, as Jesus tells us to do, (Matt. 4:4) there would be far less quarreling over what the Bible says.

We can compare the Bible to a tree, and we can compare individual verses to twigs of the branches of that tree. Now the twigs on a tree are very flexible; they can be bent various ways. So can individual verses when read out of context. They can be made to say various things that are quite contrary to each other. But we cannot bend the trunk of the tree in the same way. It stands firm and in the same place year after year. Neither can the Bible as a whole be bent to harmonize with every wind of doctrine.

Studying only certain portions here and there may have its place in a specialized study, but we should be careful not to be taken in by a study before we know something about the book or books as a whole from which such verses are taken. Beware of Bible teachers or groups who unduly emphasize some Bible verses or a portion of Scripture to the neglect of the rest of Scripture. There is an advantage in preaching and teaching from a certain book of the Bible, speaking on a portion of that book each time until the message of the book is made clear.

We often speak of feeding our soul from the Word of God. How is this done? It is done, not so much from a direct feeding, as we read and study the Bible or hear a sermon based on God's Word, although at times, when it fits our immediate need, we may benefit from such a direct feeding; but more so, we feed our soul as we draw truth from our storehouse memory in which we have stored away Biblical knowledge (Biblical truth), for that time when we will need a particular truth for a particular time in our life--such as facing a storm or crisis situation. The Holy Spirit will help us to recall it from our memory if the truth has been stored in our memory. If it has never been stored in the memory it can't be recalled.

As a life time project we need to always be filling our memory storehouse with Bible knowledge. The more of God's truth we have stored in our memories, the wiser we will be in making the right decisions and the better we will be able to face the storms of life. Our life will be built on the solid rock (Matt. 7:24-29).

Often there are times, especially when facing storms, that it is hard, even impossible, to read, study and further replenish our storehouse with more spiritual food. If at such times we have a good supply of God's truth already stored in our hearts and memories, we will have something to feed our souls on during the storm, even if we can't read and study our Bible for a time.

Too many people do not think about having food for their souls for trying times until after the storm hits. They are like the man who thinks about filling his larder with food in the dead of winter when he cannot grow a garden. It is rather late to store up soul food after the storm comes. Many who wait that long are unable to get much encouragement or help from their Bible. The best time to make hay is when the sun is shining. The best time to read your Bible and establish your faith in God is when all is going well. You will then be prepared for the storm.

There seems to be a great need for spiritual counseling in our day. Many people are perplexed. All kinds of counseling agencies are set up (some good, some bad) to help these perplexed people. Many pastors spend much of their time in individual or family counseling.

The need for all this counseling lies in the fact that the Word of God, as soul food, has not been stored in the memory or heart. Where there is good informative preaching on the truth of God's Word as a whole, and where Bible reading and studying has a place in a person's life, most of the answers to life's problems are found. As a result of God's truth stored in the heart and mind, much less, if any, counseling is needed. A pastor who continuously feeds his people richly from God's Word will find much less need of counseling those parishioners who have heard his sermons.

Such persons may become depressed but they know better how to cope with the depression, always letting God lead them through it. They learn to wait on God,

always becoming more sure that both their
waiting and their suffering are not in vain.

22. Grief

Grief is a form of depression. It is a time of acute sadness when a loved one is lost through death or other form of physical separation.

It is only natural that the person or persons left behind should feel a deep loss and be saddened. But it is unnatural if the time of grieving is prolonged, continuing on and on, and does not heal.

We may think that it is because of a very deep love bond which existed between the deceased and the person grieving that the grief does not heal. A deep bond of love may be present, yet it is not only that love as much as extreme loneliness which is often at the root of the problem. (Self-pity could also be a problem. See chapter seven.)

Or if a person should adjust very quickly after the passing of a loved one, this does not necessarily mean that the bond of love between them was not very deep.

Sometimes the person grieving does not want to make the choices and adjustments needed to fill the place the lost loved one had in his or her life. He chooces rather to bear the loneliness than to let something or someone else take the place of the lost loved one. Something or someone needs to be found to fill the deep void.

Or it may be that the person grieving just hasn't been able to find anything or anyone to take the place of the departed one who was so much a part of his or her life. It may be difficult to find that which will satisfactorily fill the void of loneliness.

Some may pour themselves into their work, a hobby, or some special interest but nothing is ever quite the same and nothing completely takes the place of the one who departed. When parents of several children lose one of their children in death they can, over a period of time, let their love for the other children fill the void--at least somewhat.

When an only child has passed away, the healing adjustment becomes more difficult. To adopt or to give birth to another child could be of help. However, in the case of a mate or child passing on, there needs to be adequate time to adjust to the loss.

If a parent or grandparent passes on, it is something that can be expected because no one is allowed to remain on this earth forever. If the children are married, they can let their immediate family fill in the void and usually the grief soon heals.

And to remarry after the death of a mate is probably the most satisfactory way to overcome the grief.

Some feel that they are being disloyal to their former mate if they remarry. But this is not the case. God, through His Word, excuses the one left behind from any and all responsibility to the deceased mate. It is not a sin for a widow or a widower to remarry. God has said, "It is not good for a man to be alone" (Gen. 2:18). The former mate no longer fills a place in the life of the one left behind, but many times adequate adjustment is made through other people or activities.

Loving and caring children can help but quite often they live far away and the grieving person does not see them often enough for them to help fill the many lonely hours he spends by himself. Close friends and neighbors can be a help, but the very best that both children and friends can do is only to partially fill the void caused by the passing of the mate.

In choosing another mate, however,

it is important that the right mate be found. The most essential thing, of course, is that the second mate be a Christian and that he or she love Jesus and His Word. But no two persons are exactly alike and some adjustments to a different kind of mate with different likes, dislikes, tastes and habits will need to be made.

When both the one who passed away and the one grieving are Christian, the grieving is much less painful. Then the grieving person is assured that they will meet again in heaven, where they will be able to be together forever without death separating them ever again.

23. Growing in Grace and Holiness

What does it mean to grow in grace and holiness? Briefly, it means to develop as a Christian, ever becoming more Christ-like. This would include a growing dislike or abomination of all sin, especially for the sin within us, with a longing to be separated from our old sinful nature, our old Adam which ever tempts us to sin.

It doesn't mean that we make resolutions such as "Don't do this," and "Do this," and then do our best to fulfill those resolutions, only to fail most miserably. Rather, we need to turn our life over to Jesus as we prayerfully (with an open mind and heart) listen to, read and study His Word, the Bible, letting Him lead and direct our life in accordance with His Word.

It doesn't mean that when we pray we act more piously, fold our hands, and bend our knees. That might help us to pray, but God does not look at our hands or knees but at our heart.

It does not mean that we pray the same prayers over and over again (Matt. 6:7), but rather that we be in the spirit of prayer at all times (I Thess. 5:17), and that after we have asked something of God, we wait on Him (Ps. 27:14) and be willing to accept whatever He wills for us. Pray as Jesus would teach you to pray (Lk. 11:1). When we pray, we need to give priority to those things that pertain to the building of God's kingdom here on earth.

When we pray for people, we need to give priority to their soul needs over their temporal and physical needs. We need to be willing to let God burden us for the soul needs of others.

It does not mean that we sing loudly or keep in tune when we sing hymns in church, but rather that our singing would express the truth that we believe and truly feel with our hearts, as well as our appreciation of what God (Jesus) has done for us. If we don't believe it, we should not sing it.

It doesn't necessarily mean that we spend more time in church, but rather that we avail ourselves of our opportunities to become better acquainted with Jesus, learning and taking to heart all that He has to teach us and allowing the Holy Spirit to be our teacher.

It means that we rejoice with those who have something good to rejoice about, and at the same time that we be ready to weep (sympathize, show love and give encouragement--let them know that we care) with those that weep.

It means that we don't try to make ourselves grow in grace and holiness but rather let Jesus have free course in our lives in causing us to grow, giving Him full credit for whatever change for the better takes place in our lives, and realizing that Jesus will never cause such change to occur if we don't really want it to happen or if we are ashamed of Him.

IV. SOME CAUSES OF CERTAIN ABNORMAL DISORDERS

24. The Hypochondriac

There are people who continuously complain of symptoms of some ailment when there is no physical evidence of any illness. They complain of symptoms which accompany a certain physical disorder or illness, and which may be very real to them, but when physically examined, they show no evidence of the illness. These persons are said to be hypochondriacs.

This does not mean that the person is pretending or faking. He may very much feel the discomforts of a certain ailment. There may be various reasons for the symptoms, but I believe one of the major reasons is that the person has a desperate need to be recognized because of loneliness and is consciously or subconsciously reaching out to be noticed. An extremely unpopular person may find that being sick or disabled is his only way to gain a bit of recognition.

I can remember, as a child, that when I was sick I received attention which I did not normally receive when I was well. I do not recall ever claiming to be sick when I was not; I cannot say that I was not tempted. And I confess that sometimes I was glad to be sick because of the sympathy and the attention I received. I can well imagine how this could be the desire of an unpopular person. With a continuing desire, which could be conscious or subconscious, and with a suspicion that you might have a certain illness, the symptoms can eventually be felt even though the illness, upon examination, is not present.

But I would like to say a bit more about the need for recognition. The statement is sometime carelessly and critically made:

"All he wants is attention." The truth is that recognition is a basic need in every person's life. It is needed for our mental health and our feeling of self worth. Life is truly miserable without it. It is sad that some people have an overabundance of popularity while others have little or none. A popular person has little need to become a hypochondriac.

The apostle Paul (I Cor. 12:23) speaks of the need of giving honor or attention to the less honorable members of a body or fellowship. We live in an age of extreme hero worship in which much honor and recognition is given to a few people, often to the neglect of others who are starving for some recognition. If this continues for a long period of time, it is apt to affect the mental health of the person who receives no recognition. He begins to feel unloved and unwanted yet still longs for some attention.

The hypochondriac may be a person who is starving for the recognition and love he badly needs. However, the way he chooses to get this need, consciously or subconsciously, by being sick, is not an acceptable way and is damaging to his social esteem and his mental health, just as stealing food is not the best way to satisfy hunger. In both cases, the method used does meet a need, but in the end causes greater problems.

When a person is suspected of being a hypochondriac, he becomes even more unpopular. Others tire of hearing his complaints and soon become indifferent to them in the hope that he might forget those complaints and not bother them. But it usually does not work that way. The hypochondriac is truly a sick person, but not in the way he thinks.

We are not on an isolated island all

by ourselves. To a large extent we live for others, and our emotional well-being thrives on their approval, especially the approval and admiration of relatives, neighbors and friends.

The healthy person will find some area, his job, some skill or hobby, his home, the way he dresses, or some other area in which to achieve. In his achievement, he draws the attention and praise of others and they encourage him to continue to achieve in that which he is good at. If he has something to sell, he is encouraged when he finds a market for his product. Sometimes he reaps criticism which tends to discourage him.

The hypochondriac is a person who either has failed to draw attention through some achievement or has never learned to achieve. Because of his need, he is often more interested in the sympathy he receives for being sick then in getting a cure for that which supposedly is his health problem. It gives him a feeling of importance.

Again, it is not wrong to want attention, but there are right and wrong ways to get it. A healthy, acceptable way is to work for it. Some people become greedy for recognition and intentionally or unintentionally rob others of recognition that should be theirs. We gain recognition when we speak up and say something in a group. Some people find it hard to make themselves heard in a group. Others may rudely monopolize the conversation, drowning out the meek and the less noticeable.

Those who have a hard time gaining recognition may become depressed. They feel unloved and unwanted. We show Christian love when we give a listening ear to those who have a harder time making themselves heard.

The hypochondriac is not as dishonest as he may seem. He is not playing sick but really does feel the pain or symptoms he complains of. However, these symptoms are not as trying to bear as the feeling of being unpopular. He has allowed his mind to play on his weaknesses and uncomfortable feelings and the recognition they bring, so he welcomes the feeling of being sick rather than being unnoticed. Because he is lonely, feels unwanted and unimportant, he is already feeling miserable and it becomes somewhat natural for him to have feelings of sickness. By letting his mind dwell on such feelings he begins to feel the symptoms of some ailment and consciously or subconsciously welcomes this because of the recognition it gives him.

We do not help those who are suffering from hypochondriac tendencies by denying them recognition. We should give it to them in an understanding, sympathetic way and by helping them to see their potential and to achieve in it. However, we need to remember that these people actually feel sick. They feel weak and may not have much physical strength because they have been dwelling on their weaknesses for so long. So the cure may be a gradual one.

We can also help such a person by looking for things in his life for which we can praise and compliment him or her--which may be only a little thing, such as the way he dresses.

However, all of those who reach out for sympathy, love and understanding because they feel sick are not hypochondriacs. Some are very depressed people who would give anything for a cure. Depressed people who complain of their depression are sometimes mistakenly thought to be hypochondriacs.

25. Neurotic Pain

Another illness which may seem much like the pain of the hypochondriac is neurosis or neurotic pain. Both sufferers feel pain when there is no physical ailment. A person suffering from neurotic pain may not be experienceing it because he feels the need to get attention. He is most anxious to get rid of the pain, recognition or no recognition.

Neurotic pain can come from continuous worry over problems for which the sufferer can find no solution. I believe it also can come from excess boredom due to idleness, or from living in regret.

In my opinion, I picture it as follows: The weary mind, tired from long periods of worry, boredom and regretful living longs for a release from this kind of thinking, so it starts to send false messages (such as pain impulses) through the nervous system, creating its own symptoms and telling itself that it is physically ill.

The mind, in order to find some release from worry and boredom, welcomes such messages created by itself and sometimes plays on them so that the pain becomes truly unbearable. This then becomes a change or release for the mind from being continuously taken up with other wearisome thoughts.

One of the characteristics of neurotic pain is that it shifts in the body. It may come from the intestinal area at one time, and from the chest or some other area at another time, causing a person to believe that he has a number of physical ailments and at the same time increasing his worry about his health.

The best help a loving friend or relative can give to such a person is:

1. Encourage him to get a complete

physical checkup so that he can be assured that nothing is physically wrong. However, often these people refuse to believe the doctor's report that nothing physically is wrong and may go from doctor to doctor hoping that one of them will find what is wrong.

    2. Try to relieve him of some of his worries and loneliness and encourage him to get involved in some way so as not to be idle, and thus have less time to think about himself. (Also see Chapter 14, entitled, "Being Idle."

26. Stress as It Relates to Certain Physical Disorders

Stress causes anxiety, and anxiety can cause depression. However, we are all different. Some people are more capable of handling their stress so that it does not develop into depression. Or certain stressful circumstances might bring depression to certain individuals, whereas that certain circumstance would not be stressful to another person; yet another type of situation would be stressful and cause him to be depressed.

Still other persons, when facing a stressful situation, might not suffer from depression at all, at least not in an acute way; but the anxiety which the stress situation has brought about eventually climaxes itself in an illness such as stomach ulcers, heart disease, high blood pressure, or asthma. However, such illnesses as these are not caused only by stress or anxiety. Other factors such as diet and life style can also cause these illnesses.

Much is still unknown as to how best to treat such ailments. Both physical and psychological treatment are often recommended. An ulcer can sometimes be cured by the right diet, but if the stressful situation which caused the ulcer is not changed, or if the patient does not learn to cope with his situation, the ulcer is likely to recur.

We can conclude that any stressful situation not dealt with properly which develops into anxiety will eventually have some ill effect on the individual. It may develop into acute depression or some psychosomatic disorder may be the result.

27. Paranoid or Bitter Feelings Toward Others

We have seen thus far that, especially in the eyes of God, depression is not always bad and that He well might will such an experience for us for various good reasons, especially in order to mature us and use us to a greater degree. Although depression is unpleasant and even painful to bear, nevertheless God will work it out for the Christian's eternal good and the good of His kingdom on earth.

However, although God intends good, in reality it does not always turn out that way. The devil tries in every possible way to interfere with God's plan and to turn into evil what God intends for good. The devil is brazen and does not hesitate to persuade whomever he can.

We have pointed out how the devil would tempt the depressed and mentally ill person to wallow in self-pity and past regrets, causing him to harden himself against all help and hope and refuse to take comfort or be encouraged. He even drives some to suicide, which is never according to God's plan.

Another work of the devil is to cause those who are extremely unhappy to take on paranoid tendencies. These sufferers imagine that the people of the world are all against them, and that even those who show kindness, love and a willingness to help may do so only because they have some selfish motive. Filled with suspicion, they tend to imagine the worst about everyone who offers help. They harden themselves and pull away from those who reach out in love and concern. They may even strike back in revenge, returning hate for love.

Such paranoid tendencies can affect an individual by degrees. If not dealt with, they can become more paranoid as time goes on. Some become so paranoid that they hate the whole world and all of mankind. They also develop an acute hatred for specific people, often to those with whom they have associated--neighbors, relatives and friends. It is often the love and help offered which has caused the suspicion and has sparked the hatred they show. If somehow the misunderstanding can be clarified, especially in mild cases, the paranoid tendencies may go away and love will take their place. However, this may not be easily done as the paranoid is often quite set in what he believes and it will take Jesus to change his attitude toward other people.

To be paranoid is characteristic of our old sinful nature. When Christian we will allow the love of Christ to saturate us and flow through us and we stand in less danger of becoming paranoid. Jesus is the best cure for the paranoid. There is nothing that will melt the hatred in the heart of the paranoid like the realization of the great love Jesus had for sinners in willingly giving His life for them.

Although the paranoid is suspicious of all acts of love and kindness, loving him is still the best way to bring him to reality and to release him from the hatred which enslaves him. It is by letting Jesus' love flow through us that the paranoid will best realize the great love of Jesus. He would expect hatred and rebuke in return for his unfriendly and hostile behavior; when he receives such treatment, he becomes all the more assured of what he already assumes--that the whole world is against him. Love alone can melt the hard heart filled with hate.

I remember talking to an extremely paranoid person. He hated the whole world and every one in it. Finally, after arguing with him for some time, I said to him "Did you know that Jesus loves you?" This seemed to impress him. It was the only thing I had said to him that he didn't argue about.

Paranoid persons often become paranoid because they have or think they have been ill-treated by some one or more persons. Such persons need to see how Jesus reacted to unjust treatment when falsely accused and crucified. Jesus never lost His calm; He prayed for His enemies while hanging on the cross.

Once a man who had been mistreated complained to me about it. Then he asked, "Is it fair that I should be treated so?"

I answered by saying: "No, it is not fair, but did Jesus ever promise that to live as a Christian would result in fair treatment? Was Jesus treated fairly?" The man calmed down and admitted that Jesus certainly had been treated very unfairly.

The hatred which a person often carries in his heart toward someone who has offended or mistreated him can be more damaging to him and cause more unhappiness, than the act of mistreatment did.

No matter to what extent we may be offended or mistreated we do well to learn from Jesus to "keep our cool" and not allow bitterness or hatred to take over in our heart. Jesus can give us grace or help to do this.

The paranoid person's greatest need is to keep bitterness and hatred from ruling in his life. This doesn't mean that he should forget all offenses and act as if no wrong has been done. This could be the worst way to deal with an offense and cause the memory of the offense to linger in the conscious or subconscious while hatred takes over the heart.

We do well to remember, as Christians, how very much Jesus has forgiven us, then ask for His wisdom as to how best to handle the situation. To face the offender calmly and coolly with his guilt often goes a long way in righting the wrong.

If this does not work, we need to remember Jesus words when He said, "Vengeance is mine" (Rom. 12:19). We can ask Jesus to take over, leaving the whole matter with Him, and resting assured that in due time He will see that justice is done. Then ask Jesus to free you from any more haunting or unpleasant thoughts about the whole matter. Ask Jesus to give you a new love for the person who offended you.

Some people think of love and trust as belonging together, and that if you really love someone you would also trust him. This is not necessarily true. We may love little children, but we do not trust them with sharp knives.

And even though Jesus loves us, there may be things we can't be trusted with. For example, if we should suddenly become very rich materially, what would that do to our love for Jesus? Would we remember His cause of missions and willingly give a portion back to Him? Or would we become so involved with many things that we wouldn't have time to sit prayerfully at His feet with our Bible and let the Holy Spirit teach us everything He would want us to know? Jesus well knows just how much of the things of this world we can take and still remain true to Him.

It is unwise to trust someone who continuously proves himself to be untrustworthy unless he has a change of heart--which could happen. But we are to continue to love the offender and pray for him. Jesus asks us to love even our enemies.

When that person, whom we considered to be our friend, proves himself to be untrustworthy and takes advantage of our love and goodness to him, it is so easy for our one-time feelings of love to turn into bitterness and hate and even thoughts of revenge.

Love could soften his greedy, sinful heart and cause him to become a different and better person. In the Bible, in Luke 19:1-10, we see what the love of Jesus did to change the heart of Zacchaeus.

When there is repentance or a change of heart, there needs to be forgiveness on our part.

There was a situation in which a pastor and his wife were badly treated by a certain lay person in their parish. Years later, when the pastor and his wife came to visit this former parish, the lay person asked for their forgiveness. But they were unwilling to forget the wrong they had suffered; they refused to forgive. This is not what Jesus would have us do when we have suffered an offense.

28. Illusions of Grandeur

Sometimes an acutely depressed person experiences periods of a very opposite feeling from depression, such as extreme happiness, optimism or hope, only to again plunge into deep feelings of depression a short time later.

I believe this could relate to the daydreaming the depressed person engages in in an attempt to find release from the depression. The mind welcomes this as an escape from continued worry and feelings of depression.

These daydreams are unrealistic. There is no way the patient can begin to work them out or make them real. After the dreams have run their course, becoming old and now rather boring--since they have taken the patient as far as they can into the dream world--the patient again relapses into depression as he comes back to reality.

An example of such a dream is for the patient to imagine that he has become the president of the United States, some great Olympic athlete setting a world record, or something similar. The patient, because of his very strong desire to be free of his depression, has trouble separating the real from the imaginative and actually comes to believe that what he is daydreaming is coming to pass. When he comes back to reality he is still depressed. His mind again takes up all the worries and concerns which caused his depression.

After a while a person who becomes accustomed to drifting off into such a dream world may lose all touch with reality. Living in such a dream world can give one temporary release from very acute depressed feelings, but it is detrimental in the long run. It is not good to lose touch with reality. When this happens the individual no longer makes any effort to plan his life realistically; he is content to live in his dream world (See Chapter 15 entitled "Daydreaming.") There is that which is good and healthy about daydreaming for one's mental health when not carried to extremes.

The New Age Movement capitalizes on this type of extreme daydreaming as it caters to the occult and the demonic world. It advocates training the mind not to think on what is unpleasant or depressing.

Some monks of the Middle Ages tried this. They locked themselves in monasteries away from the world, hoping to gain happiness and complete contentment by being separated from the world and its cares, ills, and desires as much as possible in order to think only on God and His goodness. But this is not good for mental health.

We can help the acutely depressed person by getting him to share his ambitions or dreams and then sorting out the attainable from the unattainable (or immediately unattainable), outlining realistic steps he can take to make his dream realistic. In a lesser way, we can help an individual to set his heart on some everyday enjoyments which appeal to him, showing him how he can achieve those enjoyments in a realistic way.

29. Alcoholism

Many alcoholics drink because they are depressed. Feelings such as worry, guilt, rejection, failure, or boredom lead to depression. Alcohol offers a quick escape from these undesirable feelings, but at the same time alcohol deceives. The escape is only temporary--as soon as the effects of the alcohol wear off, the old problems are back more acute than ever. More and more alcohol is needed for escape from the problems and depression.

Alcohol demands a great price for the little relief it gives. It robs one of the willpower to reason and think clearly. It silences the conscience so that one has freedom to do and say things one ordinarily does not do or say. It is damaging to one's health in a number of ways. In addition to the miserable feelings which cause the alcoholic to drink, when he sobers up he has added feelings of guilt because of what he has said or done while under the influence of alcohol. The problem grows worse instead of better. Alcohol has a way of adding its own miserable feelings to those which already exist, thus increasing the depression. The alcoholic finds it harder and harder to live with these feelings; they become unbearable, more alcohol is needed, and he finds himself in a vicious cycle. One theory concerning the drinking of alcohol is that it first gives the drinker a good "upper" feeling which is soon followed by a much intense lower or depressed feeling. And when the drinker is affected by the depressed feeling he is tempted to continue drinking in hopes that he will regain the good feeling he had when he started drinking. But drinking only aggravates the depression. I believe this to be very satanic. It is another way in which the devil deceives his victim.

If we can help the depressed alcoholic to face his problem, without relying on drink, by encouraging him to draw on God's grace, instead, for help; and to gain some self-esteem for himself and credibility with others and with God, he will feel less need to drink.

Every alcoholic starts out as a social drinker, and at this point he enjoys his drinking. He delights in what alcohol seems to be doing for him. It may make him more talkative; it becomes easier for him to be more sociable; it takes away his timidity and fear of other people. He feels a freedom to do and say things and to mix with others which he never had before he started drinking. Alcohol seems to enrich his fellowship, at least in his own eyes, making him more acceptable to others--especially if his fellowship is with other social drinkers.

It seems good to him to overcome the fears that stand in the way of becoming more sociable and more acceptable. But alcohol does not stop where it should. He gains a freedom to act in ways which will trouble his conscience later on when he is sober again. His timidity needs to be overcome with a sober mind so that he can rationally and clearly think through his actions so that he will be more acceptable to God, to others, and to his own conscience.

His fear of socializing has a purpose. It is to teach him to move carefully in a gracious, charming, loving way which is socially acceptable. When drinking he becomes like a bull in a china closet. Drinking, especially in the long run, does not build up but tears down. It destroys his character much more, than what the drinker thinks he is gaining by becoming more likeable. Drinking does not help the drinker to learn, build character, become lovable and admirable to others. Rather it makes him undesirable and repulsive. It only helps him to be reckless.

There are those who would tell us that alcoholism is a disease. Although it has characteristics similar to those of a disease, it is a sin more than a disease. The alcoholic needs to repent and look to God for grace to overcome.

Unlike a disease, it is not caused by a bacteria or a virus. It is not contagious in the same way as a disease which invades the body against the person's will. Alcohol will only enter the body and conquer the person when invited to come in. Any person who refuses to take that first drink will never become an alcoholic.

Drinking without restraint is like surrendering to the enemy. When this happens, free course is given for alcohol to enter the body and do its destructive work. The individual who drinks without restraint will slowly destroy himself.

Alcohol is no respecter of persons. Like an enemy, it will conquer the individual who allows himself to drink without restraint over a period of time. As long as restraint is exercised, the enslaving process is hindered to some extent. It is the continuing restraint used by some drinkers that prevents them from becoming alcoholics.

If alcohol once gains a beachhead and is not halted, it will continue to invade until it completely controls one's life. Once it gains hold of the individual, it is enslaving like any other disease. Many diseases, like the common cold, run their course before health is restored, but alcohol continues to become more acute as long as alcohol is taken into the body. When alcohol no longer gains entrance into the body, the ill effects will subside, but the damage done to the liver, heart and other organs could be permanent.

Unlike a disease, alcoholism is the result of every alcoholic's own doing. Many authorities claim that some people are more prone to becoming alcoholic and therefore are seemingly helpless to its onslaught, while others seem to be able to control their drinking and never become completely enslaved to the habit. They continue to emphasize that it is a disease and that the alcoholic needs to be cared for and looked upon like any other sick person. This is only partly true. An alcoholic is an alcoholic because he has sinned against his own body and mind. Once he sees his sin and repents of it, he deserves to be forgiven and helped to regain a respected place in society. It does little good to blame others or attribute it to his natural inability to resist the enslaving effects of alcohol. And although it may not have been scientifically proven, I believe that anyone who willfully throws away all restraint and drinks with the intent to become intoxicated again and again is inclined to become an alcoholic sooner or later no matter who that person is. Because of a particular makeup some might not become alcoholic as soon as others. Nevertheless, I do believe that alcoholism develops as a result of drinking without restraint.

Such a thing as a doorway to a drinking place, or an alluring advertisement in a magazine or on a billboard, is enough to start the alcoholics' drinking. Friends and loved ones may reason with them that it is foolish to drink. They will agree and sincerely vow to quit but suddenly find themselves drinking again, not realizing what caused them to start. They have little or no will to resist. Drinking becomes like an inner compulsion. The very sight or thought of drink seems to draw them to the bottle. They are not able to do otherwise even when they have good intentions. They are so enslaved they drink before they realize it.

We are told that we, as a people, did well to legalize the selling of alcoholic drinks and to tax the alcohol, thus doing away with the bootlegger, because those who want to drink will drink anyway. If they can't do it legally they will do it illegally. But I believe there are those who would like to quit, and would find it easier to quit, if alcohol were not advertised so strongly and made less available. Certainly the sale of alcoholic beverages has skyrocketed since it was made legal.

The need in curing the alcoholic of his desire to drink, after he shows signs of wanting to get rid of his habit, is to strengthen or revive his willpower so that he can resist the temptation. Friends and loved ones can help an alcoholic to regain his willpower by encouraging him not to drink each time he is tempted. This is not easy because they are not always around when strong drink allures them. It does little good to make him promise not to drink because the alcoholic is unable to resist the temptation.

But we need to back up a bit. The first step in helping the alcoholic is for the alcoholic to see and admit that he is an alcoholic who needs help. This often is not easy. But until he sees his need for help, he is not likely to accept any help. Many times all those who are acquainted with the alcoholic know that he is an alcoholic long before he realizes or admits it to himself.

We have come to believe in our society

that social drinking is no sin but even the right thing to do, or that no wrong is done until the drinker becomes an alcoholic. In view of this many an alcoholic thinks of himself as a social drinker and does not admit that he is an alcoholic because as a social drinker he has done no wrong. I believe we will experience more success in helping the alcoholic if we can help him to see that it is not only drunkenness that is a sin, and a detriment to his health, but also the use of alcohol in any form.

Proverbs 23:31-32 strongly advocates abstinence: "Look not thou upon the wine when it is red, when it giveth his color in the cup, when it moveth itself upright. At the last it biteth like a serpent, and stingeth like an adder."

The alcoholic is also made to believe that since he is an alcoholic, he is not permitted to drink, but that those who are not alcoholic have that right. This makes the alcoholic the undesirable person and the social drinker the accepted one. And so again, for this reason, the alcoholic is reluctant in admitting that he is an alcoholic rather than a social drinker because of how this would degrade him socially. He needs to see that social drinking, too, is a sin and that it leads to alcoholism.

Instead of drinking friends, a Christian fellowship, where other members are interested in the truth of God's Word, can do much to bring comfort and encouragement to the alcoholic and will help him live with his problems and learn what is the best way to deal with them.

30. Drugs and Shock Treatments

Tranquilizers, or drugs for the depressed, have been called the wonder drugs. It does seem that they give relief from depression as long as the patient continues it. But should he stop using the drug, so often the depression comes back.

One of the side effects of taking tranquilizers is listlessness, sometimes extreme listlessness which in my experience was as aggravating as the depression. It is like trading one evil for another.

Personally, I question if tranquilizers ever do much more than sedate the patient so that he can't feel the depression.

Some psychologists and psychiatrists seem to rely very heavily upon drugs in treating their patients, rather than upon counseling. There may be a couple of reasons for this.

One: Counseling is work. It is much easier just to hand out pills than to give counseling.

Two: Counselors who know Jesus and are willing to learn from Him have much more to offer in ministering to the depressed.

I would say the same thing regarding shock treatments. They do seem to give relief from extreme depression to some people. I don't believe it has ever been determined just what such treatments do to a patient, except give some relief from depression. But there is a side effect. They are known to affect the memory, especially the ability to remember names, dates and places.

It is my belief that there is a cause for acute depression with every depressed person other than chemical deficiency.

However some people are more apt to become depressed due to emotional deficiency or not having a firm hold on Christ (See chapter three).

But at the same time due to pressure from the world, much sin and evil in the world, and a burden for lost loved ones, the Christian is apt to be more susceptible to depression.

The best treatment for depression is good Christian counseling, love, patience, and encouragement. To look up to Jesus for help is truly the best remedy for depression.

Good counseling which helps the patient better understand his problem and see what he can do about it has helped patients get over their depression, whereas drugs often become a lifetime ordeal. Even though tranquilizers may not be habit-forming so that the patient craves the drugs, he, nevertheless, becomes very dependent upon them and dares not stop taking them for fear of a relapse into depression.

In ministering to the depressed one should be very careful not to make the depressed feel guilty, especially to feel guilty because he is depressed. Usually the depressed, especially if they are Christian, are already filled with guilt, and more guilt will only aggravate the situation. The big need in help for the depressed is encouragement.

V. MINISTERING TO THE DEPRESSED

31. How to Minister to the Depressed
Romans 12:15 (K.J.V.)

Romans 12:15 reads: "Rejoice with them that rejoice and weep with them that weep."

There are three truths, revealed to us in this verse, to which I would like to draw your attention.

First, we are admonished to rejoice with those who rejoice. This is the easy part of being a Christian. To rejoice means to be happy. And who does not want to be happy?

When we have something which encourages us, or gladdens our heart, we like to share it with others so that they can rejoice and be happy with us. Our joys and encouragements, that which makes us happy, seems to mean more to us when we can share them with someone, especially close loved ones.

Usually it is not too difficult to find someone to rejoice with us when we have something that brings us joy and cause for rejoicing. And if we are Christian, we truly have something to rejoice about and to be thankful for.

We praise God and rejoice because of Jesus and His great love for us, and all that He has done and promises to do for us as we give our heart to Him.

We rejoice and are glad because of how Jesus was willing to die on a cross for us--taking our place on that cross, and for His willingness to forgive us all our sins.

We rejoice and are glad because of the peace of heart and assurance of salvation which He promises to us when we let Him take our sins from us.

We rejoice and are glad because of how Jesus ever watches over us and protects us from danger.

We rejoice and are glad because of how Jesus gives grace or strength to overcome when tempted to sin.

And we are grateful for answered prayer and all encouragements which come our way in our Christian walk.

And most of all, we rejoice and are glad because of the hope of heaven and of Jesus' promise to return to earth to claim His own for heaven.

But there is more for us to consider and take to heart from this verse which tells us to "rejoice with those who rejoice." And this brings me to the second truth found in our text verse. We are also admonished to "weep with those who weep." Now to weep is the opposite of rejoicing or being happy. Oh, we speak of tears of joy but this is not the kind of weeping this verse is talking about. To weep, really weep, is to be unhappy, to be sad. It is those who are carrying a heavy heart who weep.

Now some people seem to think if we are truly Christian that Jesus wills that we be happy and rejoicing all the time and that if really Christian we should have no occasion to weep. If we are Christian, and when we get to heaven, all our tears will be wiped away and we will be happy and rejoicing all the time. We will never be sad, or have anything to be sad about or which will cause our heart to be heavy.

But that has not been promised, even to the most faithful Christians, here on earth. There is much in this world which would cause a person's heart to ache, and the heart of the Christian to ache as well.

There are some things which bring sadness to the Christian much more than to the non-Christian who usually shows less concern for those things which concern the Christian. Our text verse indicates that if we are truly Christian, with a compassionate heart, we will not only weep and feel unhappy because of our own heartaches, but we will also weep, have compassion, feel sympathetic toward others who carry a heavy heart or have serious problems in life.

And this is a hard part about being a Christian. Whereas we may find it fairly easy to find someone to rejoice with us when we have cause for rejoicing, it is not always so easy to find someone who is willing to weep with us when our heart is heavy.

I have mentioned some of the things in which the Christian can rejoice but now I will mention some of the things' which greatly sadden the Christian and cause him to weep.

One of the most depressing things for a Christian is lost loved ones who have not given their heart to Jesus. They have not confessed their sins to Him. They often love the world and the things of the world more than they love Jesus. Their conversation and actions reveal this about them.

Because they are our loved ones, and because we do love them, the thought of them possibly spending eternity in hell and missing out on all of the blessings of heaven, terrifies us and causes our hearts to be heavy.

How we wish that these loved ones would have the same concern for their soul salvation as we do. In the world in which we live there are Christian mothers and fathers who weep for their lost unsaved sons and daughters. There are Christian children who weep for their wayward parents.

There are grandparents who weep for their unsaved grandchildren. There are Christian wives who weep for ungodly husbands. There are Christian husbands who weep for their non-Christian wives. There are Sunday school teachers who weep for the children of their class. Pastors weep for the people in their parish. And sometimes the people in the pew weep for their pastor. Neighbors weep for their neighbor, etc.

If we think of ourselves as being Christian but have no soul concern for the lost all around us, then there is something wrong with our Christianity.

Jesus wept over Jerusalem because the people rejected Him and the saving grace He came to offer them. He prayed on the cross for God to forgive those who crucified Him. He didn't will that they spend eternity in hell. Jesus was deeply saddened by the world He came to save, and which rejected Him. If you haven't come to Jesus to seek His forgiveness He is waiting for you to come, and if you are a Christian, Jesus wills that you too be concerned and weep with Him for the lost in this world.

Another thing which saddens the Christian is all the ungodliness, all the sin and unrighteousness, which exists in this world. If we are Christian our hearts will ache as we see the many things all around us which are not as they should be. If we are not a Christian these things might not bother us nearly as much. We might even find joy in these things. All of the greed, coveting, selfishness, drunkenness, adultery (and the list goes on) is depressing to the Christian.

One of the most disheartening things in our day is the much aborting of unborn babies. How very much this terrible crime of murdering unborn innocent babies, which runs into the millions, must grieve God.

We might be tempted to think, "Why worry about all of these things? Why be concerned because there seems to be so little we can do to change the situation?"

Yes, it may be true, there is little we can do--at least it would seem so. But when we think of the terrible outcome, and where all of this will end--the world is headed straight for hell--it becomes our concern, because, in a Christian sense, we are our brother's keepers. Again let me repeat, if we are not concerned about the world's condition, there is something wrong with our Christianity.

We may not be able to change much in this world--especially if the world doesn't want to change. However, with God's help we must do what we can. We must warn whomever we can that the worldly are headed for hell.

There are Christians who are saddened because they are lonely. Some of them are in places where they have to stand alone in their convictions. The world seems to be rushing by them on all sides and on the broad way to its doom. These Christians stand in the gap, seemingly all alone. They know that Jesus is with them, but the world is against them, and so they feel very much alone.

Perhaps you have felt that way at times and the temptation comes to forsake your convictions and to become a part of the world in order to have fellowship and something in common with the world, and in this way become less lonely. But such an act is like selling our birthright for a mess of pottage.

This world in its madness has nothing worthwhile or lasting to offer us. We will only end up where the worldly will end up, in hell, if we join up with the world in order to have fellowship. Let us be careful that we never give in to the world, thinking the world has something worthwhile to offer us.

These are some of the heartaches that the Christian faces. Besides this he also faces the same disappointments and problems that a non-Christian faces--such as death of a loved one, ill health, financial loss, etc,.

The Christian too has feelings, even as Jesus had feelings. Disappointments and problems in life will cause the heart of a Christian to ache just as it does the non-Christian.

But not only does the Christian have his own disappointments and problems, but our text verse admonishes the Christian to also share in the disappointments, sorrows, and heartaches of others. "Weep with those that weep," it says.

Truly, my friends, there is far more involved in the Christian walk than just to rejoice. May God give us grace to also weep where and when we should be weeping as well.

But what do we mean when we speak of weeping with those who weep? And how is our weeping with them going to do any good?

To weep is to show concern and sympathy to those who carry a heavy heart. Often times we may not be able to do very much in giving help or in easing the situation for those who are hurting. To weep may be all we can do. However, we can also ask God to intervene by offering to pray for and with those who weep. But if we really care, we would like to be able to do more, if only we could.

As a pastor I have often felt so useless in trying to be a help to someone with a heavy heart. But then I realize that God does not expect me to do what I am unable to do or lack the resources needed to remedy the situation. To give sympathy and prayer support may be all I have to offer

And so I must be content to offer sympathy, prayer and some encouraging and comforting passages from God's Word, and that is all. I have nothing in myself to give.

But I have truly been amazed at times as to what extent such concern and prayer support has been a help, comfort, and encouragement to someone who carries a heavy heart. It seems so little but God uses it.

You see, when we show love, compassion and concern (such as befits a Christian) it is as if we take part of the weight of that burden upon ourselves and actually make the burden much lighter for the one who is carrying it. We don't solve the problem. We are not miracle workers, but we release the pressure, we lighten the load so that the heavy-hearted is better able to carry the load. We do this by weeping with him.

I realize how this has worked in my own life. There have been times when I have been discouraged and then received a word of encouragement from someone who cares, which has often been my wife. It has made the burden lighter. I can now carry it with greater ease. Just to know that someone cares, is concerned, makes all the difference in the world. Just to realize that someone is willing to weep with me makes such a difference.

And a Christian will always welcome prayer support, and allows himself to be comforted and encouraged by realizing that someone does care and is praying for him. By praying we contact a help, a God of power, a source of wisdom, who has a heart of compassion, and who is willing to help. When we pray, we are reaching out to God, to Jesus, who loves us and who wills only the best for us.

He promises to work it all out, not only in a way which would solve our problem, but that we will also gain in some way. He promises to work it all out for good, even our good.

When someone is willing to weep with us and pray with us--show love and concern, it gives us patience and courage to endure as long as God wills that we endure.

And our God, our Lord Jesus Christ, will either solve our problem or continue to give grace so that we can endure--whichever would be the best for us in the long run, or for our eternal good.

There are many people in this world, both Christian and non-Christian, who carry a heavy heart. This is not surprising when we realize what kind of world we are living in. There are many people who are discouraged and depressed. There is a real need for people who are willing to show sympathy for these weeping people.

Oftentimes a non-Christian is won for Christ because some Christian has been willing to weep with him or her. Jesus is in need of Christians who are willing to weep with those who are weeping.

All around us there are people who are reaching out for sympathy and understanding. They are lonely, hurt people. Many of them are confused. They are depressed. They have questions without answers They are hurting inside. They have problems to which they have not been able to find a solution.

Such people hunger for a bit of sympathy. Just to know that someone cares would mean so much to them. These people hunger for a bit of sympathy and understanding because that is what they need.

And the need is not for someone to rejoice with them because they do not feel like rejoicing. Their need is for someone to weep with them because they are weeping, weeping inside.

Just as a hungry person needs food so the lonely, depressed person, carrying a heavy heart, is reaching out for love, understanding and sympathy because this is his need. He is in need of someone to weep with him. He wants to be assured that someone cares.

The world and also the church talk a lot about love but often are very slow in giving real sympathy and to pay the price of weeping with someone.

Sympathy, real sympathy, which comes from the heart, is a product of love. It is probably the most costly way of all to show our love. And because it is costly, we do not give out sympathy carelessly. We don't give it, really give it, without counting the cost. To show sympathy is to get involved with someone's sad, unhappy feelings, and to share in those feelings.

Jesus suffered as no person ever suffered. Much of His suffering involved heartache and soul anguish for others. Jesus freely enters into the sufferings of others with His sympathy and love.

Jesus is an example for us to follow. And we need grace, we need God's help in being able to show real sympathy and love to those who are hurting. It is as we show sympathy and love for others that others are able to see Jesus in us.

Our daughter Ruth once served as a nurse at a Bible Camp for young children. She found out that a word of sympathy, with a tender kiss, was the best medicine she had to work with. It cured more ills than all of the medicines she had at her disposal.

And in just a little different way this also works with adults. Love and sympathy are the things we are to use, together with God's Word, in ministering to others.

Such sympathy and love does not solve all problems, but it can slow up the flow of tears, and ease the heartaches of the one weeping. Sympathy and prayer will lighten the load which the heavy-hearted are carrying.

Now the third truth I draw your attention to is something which the text does not say we are to do but stands as an opposite to the text and what it tells us to do.

It does not say that we are to rejoice with those that weep. And yet this is the thing many, mistakenly, are doing.

To rejoice with those that weep does not comfort, but only adds to their depression or sorrow. It causes the troubled person to wonder if anyone really cares or understands the depth of his or her problem. He wonders why he should be so sad and unhappy when everyone else, seemingly, is so happy. To rejoice with those who are weeping does not change the weeping to rejoicing but often only brings confusion. To rejoice with those that are weeping is to ignore the seriousness of their problem rather then seriously facing it. It is like having a band concert at a funeral. It just doesn't fit

I once spoke on this same text in Astoria, Oregon. And I will not soon forget the remarks of the pastor after I finished speaking.

He told of the time that his wife passed away. A friend came to him, and never said a word, but just put his arm around him and wept on his shoulder. And the pastor remarked, what comfort, what a release from sorrow, this man's weeping was to him.

JN 11:35

When Jesus came to Mary and Martha's home after the death of Lazarus, the Bible tells us that He wept. The fact that Jesus wept at this time, may be somewhat surprising to us, realizing that Jesus must have known that very shortly He would be raising Lazarus from the dead which would cause great rejoicing.

Now why would Jesus weep when He was about to bring such great joy to this group? Jesus had great compassion for the suffering and sorrowing. He identified with others in their sorrow. By first weeping with Mary and Martha, and all others who were in sorrow and weeping, He entered into their sorrow, revealing the fact that He did care, had a compassionate heart, and that He understood. He demonstrated His concern. He offered love and sympathy. He made it plain that He knew of the depth of their grief. He showed His compassion.

We can be assured that Jesus' weeping at this time was the first comfort or the beginning of the comfort which He brought to this sorrowing group of people.

And even as Jesus has identified Himself with the suffering of mankind He has also identified Himself with the sins of man. Even though He was innocent of sin, it was because of sin that He died a criminal's death on the cross.

And now Jesus would ask of the Christians that they demonstrate understanding, love and compassion toward those who weep and carry a heavy heart. And Jesus will use this to advance His kingdom here on earth.

We have much more emphasis on the need to rejoice than on the need to be willing to weep with those who are weeping. So much more, I fear, that the need to rejoice overshadows or minimizes the urgent need to weep with those that weep.

Christians, who are to bear witness of a compassionate Savior, who because of love, was willing to suffer and die in order to save sinners such as you and me, will have a much more effective witness and will be better able to demonstrate the love that Jesus has for sinners, if they learn to weep and are willing to weep with those who do weep.

A Christian witness with an over-emphasis on rejoicing (to the neglect of weeping) has a witness which only falls on deaf ears and confused hearts of those who do weep. It does not do the job. There is no meeting of heart and mind between the speaker and the listener when this happens.

There is so much emphasis on rejoicing in our day that often a stigma is attached to those who weep or have a heavy heart. Their faith, or relationship to Jesus, is often questioned if they are expressing sorrow or heaviness of heart instead of joy and a happy feeling. And because of this stigma many heavy-hearted Christians hesitate sharing their sad feelings with others. They suffer alone believing that no one really cares. In closing let me say that it is not a sin to rejoice. And if Christian, as mentioned, we certainly have cause for rejoicing. But neither is it a sin to weep. It all depends on the situation in which we find ourselves.

Paul, for example, is often thought of as the great rejoicing apostle because he rejoiced with the people of Philippi in a letter which he wrote to them while in prison.

However, when Paul wrote a letter to the Galatians and the Corinthians, he revealed that he was carrying a very heavy heart.

You see, when Paul wrote to the Philippians, he was rejoicing because the kingdom of God on earth was advancing through the efforts of this church. And Paul's being in or out of prison played no part in his cause for rejoicing.

But when Paul wrote letters to the church at Corinth and to the church in Galatia he was sad and depressed because the devil seemed to be winning the victory in these places. You see Paul rejoiced in the kind of things that God would rejoice in and he was saddened by that which he knew would sadden God.

How do you think God must feel as He looks down from heaven upon this earth which He created and loves, and sees how sin has been on the increase in so many places and in so many ways in our day?

Somehow, I can't see God sitting up in heaven with folded hands, a smile on His face, and in a continually joyous mood.

I fear that what God sees as He looks out over this world, must also anger Him and kindle His wrath. And if the situation here on earth saddens God, shouldn't it sadden us also.

I believe we should follow the example which Paul left us--that we rejoice in that which would cause God to rejoice, and that we become saddened, depressed and maybe even shed some tears when we see and experience that which we know would sadden God.

32. A Word to the Pastors

At this point I would like to say a word to the pastors who have the responsibility of bringing God's Word to their congregations on Sunday mornings and at other times.

The general spirit and atmosphere of our Sunday School hour and worship service has changed much in the past decades. The mood has become lighter and much of the seriousness once evident in our worship services is lost. Often the atmosphere is more like that of a fair than that of a setting where God is honored, respected and shown reverence. The appeal is to the emotions and the whole program is far less edifying than formerly.

This atmosphere has been ushered in, at least in part, by the charismatic movement and also by the Church Growth Movement, which have had their influence upon all of Christendom. The introduction of light, catchy gospel songs and music with a great deal of rhythm amd swing has helped bring about this change. It is considered less important that our hymns be edifying and God-centered. The music often becomes more important than the message of the words. Sometimes it is all that can be heard.

"Love" is greatly stressed. Love is important but, at the same time, "truth" and other virtues are being neglected when only love, together with loud band-like praise, are continuously emphasized. As good and as appealing as this kind of emphasis may seem to be, the result is to make our worship service more of an entertainment than a serious learning of God's Word.

There is much talk about the need for revival. Do we think that this kind of worship which appeals to the emotions will

- 169 -

change the heart more quickly and better than an edifying program which goes deep into God's Word? Is it not true that the power to change lives lies in the power of God's Word when clearly taught and proclaimed? Or do we think that this kind of light, entertaining type of worship is revival, a sign of spiritual life in the church? I fear some people think so. If there is not this kind of fair-like atmosphere in the church, they conclude that the church is spiritually dead. It is true that there may be a lot of spiritual deadness in the church, but a loud, entertaining type of worship service is no sign that spiritual life is present.

A thorough preaching and teaching of God's Word and the clear presentation of its complete truth will do more to bring revival than appealing to the emotions ever will. True revival is characterized not by much noise, but by true repentance of sin and a changed life as a result of hearing and accepting God's truth.

Our worship services should show recognition and concern for the depressed. Our pastors should be more sympathetic and encouraging to these weary warriors of the cross. Too often the depressed Christians are made to feel guilty because they are depressed and weary and do not feel like taking part in the festive spirit of the congregation. They dare not express their problems when the spirit of the day is loud rejoicing.

There is a great need in today's preaching to recognize the cross that Jesus wants His own to carry. We need to assure those Christians who suffer that they do not suffer in vain. We need to present Jesus as one who suffered and wept, so that those who are weeping can identify with this side of Jesus. We need to make it clear that God tests the faith and loyalty of His own in order to prepare them for greater use in the Christian warfare, and that these testings, which may take the form of suffering or depression, are not a punishment for sin (John 15:2b). We also need to assure these weary Christians that Jesus will never leave them nor forsake them (Heb. 13:5), but that He does give help and grace for every trial and testing (Matt. 28:20).

God's house is not only a place to convert the ungodly to Christ and gain new recruits for the warfare. It is not only a place where we see our sins as Christians. It is not only a place in which we express praise and thanksgiving to God. Granted, these emphases are certainly essential. Love is a great virtue, but there is a cost to love as Jesus loved, and love is not the only virtue Jesus wills to see in us. The church should also be a place where the weary Christian involved in the Christian warfare can be strengthened from God's Word and given encouragement to continue on in that warfare.

The Christian warrior comes to church with a need. He questions, "Why did this happen to me?" He needs a word of encouragement in his Christian warfare. We needs to be assured and reassured that storm and tribulation in the life of the Christian are normal, not abnormal, and that God will work it all out for good in due time (Rom. 8:28). He needs a greater understanding of God's Word which will give answers to the questions he faces in relation to his problems. A constant fare of loud, jubilant praise to God aggravates his problem and fails to meet his need. It leaves him confused rather than enlightened.

33. Uncovering the Subconscious

Each of us has a storehouse of knowledge somewhere in the brain or mind. We call it memory. Many things in this memory bank we can bring into our conscious thinking whenever we will. But some things that we know seem to be locked up in a vault in our memory. We need some kind of reminder closely associated with what we are trying to remember, and this reminder serves as a key to unlock the vault to bring that knowledge into conscious thinking.

This vault is sometimes called the subconscious. It is like a vault with a vast filing system in which knowledge is stored. Each file needs its own key, or reminder, in order to release its information for present use. Some facts, or bits of memory, are buried deep in the files of the subconscious. Sometimes it is difficult to find the right reminder, or key, to unlock the files and bring into conscious memory the information we desire or need.

We speak of forgetting or vaguely remembering some things. We are able to relearn some things we once knew much more quickly than we learned them· the first time. The reason is that we never really forgot them; they have been deeply buried in the file of our subconscious. All that is needed to relearn what we once knew is to find the right reminder-key to bring them into our conscious memory. We tend to lock up those thoughts or memories that we have no use for at the present.

But sometimes there are things which we want to forget because thinking of them depresses us, or causes us to fear. Since we want to forget them, we tend to lock them in our memory vaults. This act is sometimes referred to as pushing it into the subconscious. Such thoughts might include anything that makes us feel guilty, some responsibility we are trying to evade, things we are afraid of, some trying experience, or anything else we would rather not face at the present moment. However, such matters do not remain locked up in the memory vault. We continuously run into things which remind us of them and which serve as a key to release them from the subconscious and bring them into the conscious.

The mind does not always seem to have a good way of taking care of this problem. It tends, over a period of time, to lock some thoughts securely in the subconscious so that no other thought will easily bring them back into memory. And if the thoughts which have been securely locked away have a depressing effect upon us when in conscious memory, they tend also to depress us when in the subconscious memory vault, and they continue to have a damaging effect upon our mental health and emotional stability even though we do not consciously think about them any longer.

A psychiatrist or psychologist who is trained to deal with such things knows how to open up these securely locked memory vaults and bring the thoughts stored there into the conscious memory. The deeply depressed person is helped to face his thoughts as they need to be faced so they can either remain in the conscious memory without upsetting him or be stored in the memory vault without festering and threatening his mental health.

It is unwise to lock in the memory vault unpleasant thoughts which should be dealt with. Such thoughts do not remain dormant in the subconscious but continue to fester as a threat to the emotional and mental health. The thoughts are like canned fruit not properly prepared, which will only spoil and be a problem rather than an asset.

If guilt is involved, we need to confess our fault and seek forgiveness. If we are uncertain of guilt, we need to find out. If there is a responsibility to face, we should face it. If there is something we do not completely understand but need to know more about, we should seek such knowledge. If there is something we fear, we need to know how threatening it is, then do what we can to remedy the danger. Just to know the full truth will make haunting thoughts tolerable and less threatening.

Sometimes a depressed person does not know why he is depressed. In such cases it may be that he has some unpleasant thought, as mentioned above, locked securely in his memory vault which has not been properly dealt with. It lies festering in his subconscious, continuously damaging his emotional health and causing acute depression.

It may not always be necessary to unlock the subconscious in order to bring healing to the acutely depressed person, but to do so can hasten the healing. Healing from depression often comes over a period of time even though the cause or causes are not discovered. Our emotional makeup has a way of adjusting and healing itself. Time is a great healer both physically and emotionally.

There quite often are a number of causes for acute depression. Usually there is a main cause and other minor contributing causes. It seems that little, everyday unpleasant things in life, which a well person is able to cope with, add weight and aggravate the condition of those suffering from acute depression. If the main cause can be found and dealt with properly, the patient will become emotionally strengthened and better able to cope successfully with the minor causes which contributed to the depression.

During the time I was suffering from acute depression, I was unable to discover the causes. Not until I was well on the road to recovery and could look at the whole experience as something distant in my past was I able to see the main cause as well as contributing factors which brought on the depression.

Some patients seem to become very depressed over the stresses of everyday life. It may be that they have had an overly protected past and never learned to adjust to stress; then suddenly they are on their own and panic, becoming depressed.

But there are many depressed people who know what is depressing them--for example, a wife living with an alcoholic husband, or some similarly obvious situation. In such cases we do not look for the causes in the subconscious; we study and analyze the situation to see what can be done to change it. Often the solution is not easy to attain. However, we do well to bring the whole situation to God in prayer and patiently wait for Him to lead the way, working with Him in doing what we can do.

VI. GOD USES SUFFERING FOR GOOD

34. How Christian Joy and Suffering Relate

Many of today's writers and speakers describe Christian joy as something above (or free of) the storm, tribulation, sorrow, trial or testing which plague this world. They describe the mature Christian as being so filled with joy that no stressful situation would greatly affect his feelings or cause his spirit to be downcast. As a mature Christian he is supposed to be able to live above those situations. They picture Christian joy as a sort of "opiate" which deadens the pain of facing the trials of life.

But this description is not true to the Christian way of life as taught by Jesus in His Word. The truth is that if we choose to go all the way with Jesus, we truly expose ourselves to a certain type of suffering and testing which we could escape if we chose not to follow Him.

A true Christian does not follow Jesus in order to escape trial. He willingly faces trial in order to follow Him, all out of gratitude and love for Him. The hymn writer expresses it very well when he says:
"Nearer, my God, to Thee, nearer to Thee!
E'en though it be a cross that raiseth me,
Still all my song shall be,
Nearer, my God, to Thee......"

But Jesus also spoke of lasting peace and joy. What did He mean? First of all, we need to note that this lasting peace and joy relate much more to our eternal life in heaven than to life here on earth. Jesus said that here there would be tribulation (John 16:33).

Christian joy, according to the Bible, is more than a present good feeling. It is deeply rooted; it does not change as feelings do. It is a surety that God is with us and will help us and see us through every situation no matter how stressful, as long as we do not forsake Him. It is not a guarantee of a stress-free life in this world, nor is it a state of being above all stressful situations.

True Christian joy is the kind of feeling a soldier has when in the thick of the battle, knowing that his country is behind him supplying him with all he needs to fight the battle effectively, no matter how uncomfortable his immediate surroundings or how hopeless the situation might seem from his present position in the battle.

A Christian soldier of the cross, truly dedicated to Christ, is not going to ask for an easy place in the battle against sin and evil. He knows that to suffer for Christ is often needful in order that the battle can be won. He finds joy not in his present feeling but in knowing that Jesus considers him worthy to suffer for His sake. However, the suffering in itself is far from being a joyous experience.

The fruits of the Spirit, as found in the life of the Christian and listed in Galatians 5:22-23, include both joy and longsuffering. Both are found in the true Christian. While God gives joy and happiness, life is far from being all joy as we usually think of joy. There is also suffering to be endured, sometimes for a long period of time.

But the joy the Bible speaks of also manifests itself in another way--through service to Jesus. I think of my own experience and how it has worked for me, for example, when receiving a new responsibility to do something for Jesus--say, to preach a sermon on a difficult portion of Scripture in a new place. As the time draws near to preach, I feel the very opposite of joyous. Everything I do seems to take twice the ordinary effort. I have no appetite and would just as soon skip the meal preceding the appointed time. I hope the car will start but fear it might not. I hope I do not have car trouble on the way, or that something else does not cause me to be late. I hope the weather holds and that the people will not forget to come. All kinds of thoughts cross my mind, bringing a host of worries with them. I wonder if I will reach the pulpit. Sometimes I sense a tightness in my throat and wonder if my voice will hold out, or a tightness in my chest and wonder whether I might have a heart attack before I am through. I could go on and on listing my worries at such a time.

But most of these things have never happened. If something hinders my going at this point, there has always been a way around, over, under or through the hindrance. Once I start preaching, the battle seems to be won and I preach with great ease.

Following the sermon, someone often tells me that it was a blessing or help, or I am somehow assured that by God's grace I came through, winning the battle. Immediately my spirits are lifted. All that was dragging me down before has disappeared and no longer worries me. I suddenly feel joyous, also hungry and ready to eat. Sensing that God has been with me, helping me, and using me brings a good, joyous feeling. I realize also that it was well worth the heavy feeling I had entering the pulpit to experience the good feeling now. I am ready to do it all over again. But it doesn't last, I find that the joy from one such experience of service rendered to Christ soon wears off. I long for an opportunity to preach a sermon for Jesus again and to be instrumental in bringing a blessing to still more people. In anticipation of the blessing and joyous feeling I will receive, I am ready to go to the effort again of carefully preparing a message, waiting out the time to deliver it, and again facing all the worries that assail me on my way to the pulpit. Somehow I know God will see me through again as He has done so often in the past, but the worries always assail me nevertheless.

But as thrilling as it is to have this kind of joy, it is nevertheless a joy that affects my feelings, and feelings do not remain the same. Before the joy there is pain. There is anxiety and depression. There is a price to pay before a reward is realized.

In Matthew 11:28 Jesus speaks of a rest for those who labor. But notice that it is to those who have labored, not to the one who is idle, that this rest is promised. I believe it is this kind of rest Jesus gives me after I obediently prepare and preach a sermon.

There are at least two kinds of joy--the joy of the Christian and the joy of the world. The joy of the world rides on the surface of our lives. It is dependent upon feelings in order to exist. It thrives on the moment, it is not concerned about the future, and it learns nothing from the past. It is shortlived and is soon overcome by regret. Such joy is never very deep. It rides high on the waves of the sea of life and is easily overturned.

On the other hand, Christian joy is deep, like the ocean. On the surface there often are storms, even violent storms. We are told that when the waves are high and the ocean in turmoil because of high winds, only a short distance below the surface the water is calm. The storm does not disturb the deep water.

The storms of life likewise cannot penetrate deeply into the joy and security the Christian senses deep within. On the surface there may be storms, tears and a frown, but deep within there is peace. On the other hand, the non-Christian might have joy for the moment because he is willing to sacrifice all for the pleasure he can realize at the present moment. Like Esau, he is ready to sell his birthright for a mess of pottage.

The real joy for the Christian is in the hope of heaven where there are no tears or sorrow. He lives in anticipation of this hope. The nonChristian has no such hope. The Christian also realizes that heaven is not on earth and is ready to accept earth for what it is, not expecting too much. He is like a traveler going home on a cold, wintry night. He feels the cold, but the thought of a warm fire awaiting him at home warms his heart and inspires him to push onward as each step brings him closer to home.

I will never forget what our daughter Ruth said as a young girl when hoeing sugar beets for wages. "It is hard work," she said, "and I feel like quitting. But then I think of the paycheck I will get if I continue and that encourages me to keep going."

It is the sure hope of heaven which keeps the Christian steadfast in his Christian walk. I remember what Chaplain Lloyd Nelson at the Veterans Hospital in Sioux Falls, South Dakota, told me when I was a patient there. "All I want out of this life," he said, "is to hear Jesus say to me at the end of my life, 'Well done, thou good and faithful servant.'" And this word is all that really matters. Everything else is in vain. Only what we do for Jesus will last.

Therefore, if I can do something in this life which is pleasing to Jesus (such as helping others to see Him more clearly or get a blessing from His Word through my preaching, writing, or person-to-person contact), then I feel in my own heart that the inner peace and satisfaction which I am experiencing at such a time is God's way of telling me that He is pleased with what I have done. I know it is not a feeling that I have triggered in my own life. I cannot make it come by my own will. Nothing else I do gives me that same feeling. Therefore, I believe it comes from God. And it is this kind of feeling I also desire for others as they serve the Lord in an uncompromising way. Nothing compares to it. It is a peace which passes all understanding (Phil. 4:7).

The Christian joy of which the Bible speaks has its roots in storms, suffering and sorrow. "In the world ye shall have tribulation" (John 16:33b). "We must through much tribulation enter into the kingdom of God" (Acts 14:22b). It is not for us to say how much or how little tribulation we are to bear. That is up to God, and we must learn patience.

We hear people say that although they have had a sorrowful, depressing experience, they just claimed one of God's rich promises from His Word and the trying experience left them. I do not wish to doubt their experience. Very likely this is how it was for them. But sometimes they feel that everyone else who is being tried should experience the same kind of quick release by claiming the same promise. God does not give the same experience to everyone.

He does not work the same way in everyone's life. He has a reason for asking His own to endure. Our concern should not be that the sorrow and depression be lifted quickly, but that it accomplish its full purpose in building and extending God's kingdom on earth, both in our lives and in the lives of others. We can take comfort in the fact that as Christians we do not suffer in vain.

Let our prayer request in relation to suffering not only be for healing but for patience and grace to endure. In the Garden of Gethsemane Jesus did not pray for a shortcut in His suffering. He revealed a willingness to drink all of the bitter cup of suffering which God willed for Him if need be. Should not this be an example for the true Christian to follow?

The joy of the Christian has its roots in sorrow. No one goes directly to heaven. It is necessary and according to God's will that we first live our life, whether long or short, here on earth.

We realize from God's Word that we are all sinners. Each of us is born of sinful parents and has inherited a sinful nature. We also know from the Word that all sorrow, testing and suffering are directly and indirectly the fruit of sin. But we must also realize that suffering itself is not sin. Jesus did not sin before He suffered and did not sin when He suffered. He disgraced Himself before the world by suffering, but He did not disgrace Himself before His father in heaven by suffering. His suffering greatly pleased the Father.

Because we are sinful, suffering helps us to mature as Christians. Our suffering serves to make us more Christlike. God also uses our suffering to draw others to Himself, even as He used Jesus' suffering, especially when we face our suffering in an uncomplaining way.

Suffering is the result of sin, and suffering is also the way out of sin. Jesus suffered first so that we could be released from sin, but we too are asked to suffer in order to grow in grace and holiness and overcome sin. Our suffering is used by God to point others to Jesus. The narrow road has never been paved; it is hard, rough and steep. When we surrender our lives to Jesus He forgives our sin. We become justified before God. Justification is God's doing and involves no cost or suffering on our part, but after we are justified we need to be sanctified. We need to grow as Christians, and growth often involves suffering.

After Jesus ascended into heaven, He left the responsibility of building God's kingdom on earth with His disciples. The commission involved suffering on their part, but they rejoiced that they were counted worthy to suffer (Acts 5:41). Suffering is a part of the Christian way of life. But the joy of a Christian rests in the fact that he does not suffer in vain, and that some day he will come to the end of all suffering and will be with the Jesus he loves, in heaven forever where there will be true joy.

Let me hasten to say that God often gives the true Christian some very joyous mountaintop experiences. It is not wrong to hope and live for these. My own life has been a life of suffering, but it has not been without times of experiencing great joy. We can readily accept whatever such experiences of joy God gives us as our privilege as His children. The important thing is that we have the right attitude toward suffering and that we realize that our suffering is not without purpose.

35. The Cost of Following Jesus
(A Sermon Based on Mark 8:31-34)

"And He (Jesus) began to teach them that the Son of man must suffer many things, and be rejected of the elders, and of the chief priests, and scribes, and be killed, and after three days rise again. And He spoke that saying openly. And Peter took Him, and began to rebuke Him. But when He had turned about and looked on His disciples, He rebuked Peter, saying, Get thee behind me, Satan: for thou savourest not the things that be of God, but the things that be of men. And when He had called the people unto Him with His disciples also, He said unto them, Whosoever will come after me, let him deny himself, and take up his cross, and follow me."

Here we see Jesus teaching. He was a very good teacher who had a way of making Himself understood. He had wise and practical things to teach, and He taught only the truth. What He taught was pertinent to the day in which He taught and to every other day and age, including the present.

It was a hard lesson that Jesus was teaching on this particular day. It was a teaching which many people, including those especially close to Him, like His disciples, did not want to hear and accept. Nevertheless, it was a teaching which was most important for all true followers of Jesus to know and believe in relation to their discipleship. It involved the high cost of following Jesus all the way.

Jesus was trying, with a great deal of difficulty, to make clear to his listeners that He was going to suffer ridicule, persecution and crucifixion and was going to be rejected by prominent religious people like the elders, chief priests and scribes.

It would be these religious leaders who would first of all see to it that He was put to death. His death would be a most humiliating death, the death of a criminal. He would be executed on a cross for all to see.

The people who heard this Word about Jesus that day, especially His disciples, loved and respected Him and did not want these things to happen. We can appreciate this concern in Jesus' disciples. It indicated that they had a love for Jesus. You and I would have reacted in the same way if we had heard that a terrible death faced a dear friend of ours. Such a concern is not wrong. It is good when we have compassion for others.

But Jesus knew the hearts of all who were listening to Him that day, and He knew the hearts of His disciples. Even though there was love for Jesus in their hearts, there were some selfish motives as well. Jesus directs Himself to these selfish motives. These people, including Jesus' disciples, had indicated that they wanted to follow Him. They wanted to make Him their leader, but for selfish reasons. There was great potential in Jesus as a successful leader, even a political Leader. They would have liked to make Him their king (John 6:15). He had power to do great things. He demonstrated a great deal of knowledge and wisdom. He seemed to have a compassion for the poor and lowly.

The disciples wanted Jesus to succeed as their leader, because if He succeeded as a leader, perhaps even as a world ruler, they as followers had hopes of sharing in the spoils. These people had a Santa Claus concept of Jesus, and a good Santa Claus will deliver all that is asked and desired.

But, if it happened as Jesus was telling them, that He would not succeed as they hoped but would die a criminal's death, all hopes and dreams of success for Jesus and for themselves would be ruined. Their expectations for Jesus would not be realized; they would be disappointed in Him.

But Jesus' teaching is clear. He does not compromise the truth He is emphasizing. He offers no alternatives. It is as if He is saying: "You may follow me if you wish, but you must realize that it will not be as you imagine. There will not be any reaping of the kind of spoils you are hoping for." To their disappointment Jesus was not going to be the great success they had hoped He would be, but the very opposite. He would be an utter failure by their standard of success.

Jesus is honest and truthful, as He always is. He did not want these people to have any false hope of what He would do for them. Jesus does not want anyone to have the wrong idea about what it is to follow Him only to be disappointed because He is not what they expected. He does not wish to deceive them into thinking He is leading them into the kind of glory and riches they expect. Jesus was going to have to suffer and die for the sins of man in order that man might have a chance to get to heaven. The way would be costly and disgraceful, and there would not be much applause.

At this point we see Peter begin to rebuke Jesus (v.32). It was not the way Peter had imagined. To deliberately choose to go the way of suffering and death, and to allow such suffering and death in such a disgraceful way without any resistance, being branded as a criminal by respectable religious leaders like the priests and scribes, did not make sense to Peter. Neither does it makes sense to a lot of people of this world. To give without the thought of gaining something on this side of the grave seems like utter foolishness.

Jesus in return rebukes Peter and tells him that he (Peter) is being used by Satan to tempt Jesus not to go the way of the cross. I believe it was because Peter had selfish motives at this time in his early walk with Jesus that he denied Him on the morning of His crucifixion. Peter first saw Jesus as a way to fame and material gain. Jesus disappointed Peter; the end result was that Peter denied Him. Later, Peter repented. But it was not easy for Peter to accept a Jesus whose will it was to be a failure in the eyes of the world in order to save man from sin.

Satan wants to come to you and me as he did to Peter, tempting us to forsake Jesus who chooses to go the way of the cross rather than fill our desires with the comforts and pleasures of this life on earth.

After rebuking Peter Jesus bids every one to come closer. He has still more to say about the way of the cross which He chose to travel (v.34). It is as if Jesus is saying: "In spite of what others say, and in spite of what you may wish the truth to be, here are the cold facts: Whosoever will come after me, let him deny himself, and take up his cross and follow me."

In the words of today's English which we can better understand, it is as if Jesus is saying: "I must tell you honestly that if you truly wish to follow me, you will not have an easy time of it. If you follow me, not only I will have a cross to bear but the same will be expected of you. You will be denying yourself many of the things of this life which you had hoped I would gain for you, and you will suffer affliction and hardship as well."

Peter could not accept Jesus' going the way of the cross; but now Jesus also added that Peter, too, as well as all true followers, would suffer. Their experience would be the very opposite of the success and glory that they had imagined following Jesus would bring.

Two conditions are involved in following Jesus: (1) the forsaking of sin and the denying of earthly comforts and pleasures; (2) the willingness to take up the cross and suffer ridicule and persecution for Jesus' sake. So it must be if you hope to follow Jesus all the way to heaven.

The true Christian should give up any ambition to gain worldly fame and riches if it interferes with bringing glory to Christ. He would make glorifying Jesus his first ambition (Matt. 10:37-38). He does not think so much while here on earth of what Jesus will do for him now, but rather of what he can do for Jesus. He lets the hope of heaven, not the things of this world, be his present joy. Whatever he has in the way of talent, ability, physical strength, youth, vigor, material possession, and time he gladly spends in a way that will glorify Christ. If he has nothing left for himself, that does not matter.

Though we increase in physical and material ways for a time, the end result is that we decrease on this earth and leave everything behind. To follow Jesus means that we spend what God has entrusted to us in such a way that the decrease glorifies Him. It means to give rather than receive; the receiving will be in the life to come. It means to give, use or invest all that God has entrusted to us in such a way that God's kingdom on earth will go forward and grow. The life of the unbeliever decreases as well but is only wasted.

Many people live as if Jesus was the only one who ever needed to carry a cross. It is true that you and I cannot die for anyone's sins. Only Jesus could do that, and that was on the cross on which He was crucified. But in order for the full truth of the gospel to reach all people of all ages, the Christian also must take up a cross and suffer for Jesus' sake.

Again, we continuously hear that it is a smile and joyful appearance that will entice others to accept Christ. How very deceiving! It is the blood of the martyrs and the Christians' willingness to be persecuted for Christ's sake and for righteousness' sake which has impressed the lost to accept Christ. And when they come to Christ through such a witness, they already know that it is not an easy way filled with worldly benefits which they are choosing to go. They know that there will be cost, self-denial, and a cross to bear. They see how those who have witnessed to them of Jesus are already paying the price. An example from the Bible is when Paul (Saul) witnessed the stoning of Stephen.

The gospel when proclaimed in its full truth engenders opposition. The evil forces of this world do not want the truth to be proclaimed. Therefore, spreading the gospel is a warfare, and all wars are costly to those engaged in them.

In Jesus' day, as the truth spread that He had ambitions other than satisfying worldly desires, His popularity went down. Many turned from following Him. The disappointment felt by those who had hopes of gaining in a material way through Jesus turned into a hatred so intense that it nailed Him to the cross as a total outcast. These early followers of Jesus who turned against Him because He refused to bless them with earthly success and riches were like the disappointed laborers in the parable of the workers in the vineyard (Matt. 20:11), who were disappointed in the wage and began to murmur against their employer, who symbolized God. The wage they were to receive symbolizes eternal life, but they wanted something more.

In our present day and within the last decade or so, Jesus has again gained in popularity as He did during the early part of His ministry. Many more people are now speaking of Jesus and praising Him. But what kind of Jesus do they have in mind? Today's pulpits are filled with "joy prophets" who speak only of the joy and good feeling that comes to the Christian.

Again, a large number of people are looking to Jesus as a kind of Santa Claus who will miraculously cause only good (as man sees good) to come their way. Little or nothing is being said about the cross of the Christian. When the people of our day find out that Jesus is not the Santa Claus they hoped He would be, and that there is a cost involved in following Him all the way, will they turn from Him too? (Matt. 7:21-23).

The Bible speaks of a great tribulation period during the end times (Matthew chapter 24; Book of Revelation). How well will all the "joy preaching" we hear today prepare the people for such tribulation? Will it confuse them and cause them to turn from Jesus when the storm strikes? "When the Son of man (Jesus) cometh, shall He find faith on the earth?" (Luke 18:8).

According to Jesus' own teaching, the reward of the Christian is heaven, but on earth there will be tribulation (John 16:33). Ever since Jesus walked on this earth, and before, many have found the gospel truth to be offensive. The idea of suffering death in a disgraceful way, rather than choosing to succeed as the world thinks of success, is what makes it offensive.

We might be tempted to think that if the whole world could just hear the truth of God's great love for man in a way in which they can comprehend it, then everyone would accept and all would be saved. Some believe this and take for granted that all who sit under the preaching of the gospel as they interpret it will be saved.

But the truth is that the Word of God divides. "For the Word of God is quick, and powerful, and sharper than any twoedged sword, piercing even to the dividing asunder of soul and spirit, and of the joints and marrow, and is a discerner of the thoughts and intents of the heart" (Hebr. 4:12).

Jesus said that He and the truth He proclaimed would be a stone of stumbling rather than a Savior to many. "Unto you therefore which believe he is precious: but unto them which be disobedient, the stone which the builders disallowed, the same is made the head of the corner. And a stone of stumbling, and a rock of offense, even to them which stumble at the word, being disobedient: whereunto also they were appointed" (I Peter 2:7-8).

When the truth about Jesus becomes known, that He is not a Santa Claus handing out worldly goods, many reject Him and bring God's wrath upon themselves.

Many attempts have been made to improve or doctor up the truth of God's Word in order to make it more appealing to man. But we cannot improve the truth. We must accept the truth as it is, whether we like it or not. The truth cannot be changed. Any attempt to change it will spoil it and create an untruth. It is because the truth of Jesus is offensive to many that new and strange doctrines are ever coming into being. Some of these false teachings gain large followings, but they only represent man's attempt to improve the truth. It is not that man cannot understand the simple gospel truth of Jesus, that He died for the sins of man, but it is that man does not want to understand, and Satan blinds his eyes to the truth.

These new and strange doctrines invented by man are very appealing. They may even appear to be an improvement over the true gospel. They do not ask for self-denial and the forsaking of sin. They do not speak of a cross for the Christian. Instead, they offer some appealing benefits, like a God who does not want you to be sick or unhappy ever again and who will prosper you materially and give you your every desire--all in exchange for faith on your part.

The book, "Pilgrim's Progress," by John Bunyan, tells of the struggles and temptations Christian faced as he traveled the narrow road to heaven. At one point on this narrow, steep, hard road Christian met Mr. Worldly Wise. Mr. Worldly Wise convinced Christian that there was an easier way than the narrow road to heaven. Christian believed Mr. Worldly Wise and took his counsel, but found that the road proposed was not as Mr. Worldly Wise told it. It did not lead to heaven but came to a dangerous dead end. Christian almost lost his life and his soul before making his way back to the narrow road.

Satan well knows that the way of the cross is the only way to heaven; but if he can divert us from this way, still causing us to believe that we are on our way to heaven, he will have accomplished his purpose.

Jesus did not come into this world in order to make it a better place to live. He came to tell us of a better world and to encourage us to support His cause of spreading the good news of His coming to save mankind from his sin.

Jesus said: "Whosoever will come after me, let him deny himself, and take up his cross, and follow me" (Mark 8:34).

VII. MEN AND WOMEN WHOM GOD TESTED
36. Some Whom God Tested

God does put His own to the test. He will test their faith, their love for Him, and how willing they are to stand firm on their Christian convictions.

John 15:2b says: "And every branch that beareth fruit, He (God) purgeth it, that it may bring forth more fruit."

However, God offers grace or help to whomever He tests or purges so that they will be able to stand the testings--that is, if they will to stand. Some there are who fail the test, losing their faith in God in the testing.

The great men and women of the Bible were all put to the test. It was this testing which made them great.

Abel, the first human being to enter heaven, remained faithful unto death as he faced an angry, jealous brother who killed him.

Noah faced much ridicule from his neighbors, as he warned them of a coming flood. He faithfully worked for years building a big ship on dry land far from any large body of water, all because God told him to.

Abraham dared take steps toward sacrificing his only son, Isaac, whom he dearly loved, when God commanded him to do it.

Job remained true to the Lord God, even though he lost all of his possessions and family and was afflicted with painful boils.

Joseph remained faithful and true to God throughout his lonely boyhood years when forced to leave home because his brothers sold him into slavery. He continued to remain faithful when wrongly accused of adultery and sent to prison.

Moses refused the comforts and riches

of Pharaoh's court in obedience to God's will for him, and in order to lead God's people through the wilderness.

Rahab dared befriend and protect godly spies at the risk of her own life.

David risked his own life in order to protect God's people and in order to bring glory to God. He dared face the giant Goliath. He remained faithful to the Lord God as he lived in exile because of jealous King Saul who wanted to kill him.

Naomi had great sorrow because of the loss of her husband and two sons, but she remained faithful to her Lord.

Ruth chose to worship the Lord God, even though He was a God who tested His own, rather than a false heathen god.

Elijah remained faithful to the Lord God even when it seemed that everyone else was worshiping the false god, Baal.

Daniel faced the lion's den because he was not ashamed of the Lord God. He dared pray to God even though the law of the land forbade him to do so.

Nehemiah was willing to leave the comforts of the king's court where he was the king's cupbearer in order to be obedient to God's will in helping God's people who were having a very trying time in Jerusalem.

Jeremiah was greatly saddened because his people, God's people, continued to reject their God and to go against His will for them.

Esther risked her life as she faced the king in defense of her people and to the glory of God.

Jesus suffered a cruel death on the cross in order to save repentant sinners from their sins.

Jesus' disciples were beaten and finally put to death, but they remained faithful, glorifying Jesus, to the very end.

Mary trusted God for her every need

and protection although she had no place but a stable where she could give birth to God's son.

Jairus believed Jesus' promise to heal his daughter, who was critically ill, even when there was much delay in Jesus' finally getting to her bedside.

Paul endured beatings, shipwreck and many trying circumstances as he continued to proclaim Christ to the Gentiles.

And there were many more.

If God tested these beloved, faithful people of the Bible, we can expect, if Christian, that we also will experience testings at times--perhaps more so than what we anticipate.

However: His "grace is sufficient" (II Cor. 12:9).

37. Job, Jeremiah, and Elijah
(A Sermon)

When thinking about a Bible person who was extremely discouraged our thoughts might turn to Job and the Book of Job. Job was a mature man of God who became very discouraged and depressed.

For our text, I will read several portions from the book of Job. First, chapter 1, verse 1.

"There was a man in the land of Uz, whose name was Job; and that man was perfect and upright, and one that feared God, and eschewed evil."

And then skipping down to verses 8 through 12.

"And the Lord said unto Satan, Hast thou considered my servant Job, that there is none like him in the earth, a perfect and upright man, one that feareth God, and escheweth evil?

"Then Satan answered the Lord and said, Doth Job fear God for nought?

"Hast not thou made an hedge about him, and about his house, and about all that he hath on every side? thou hast blessed the work of his hands, and his substance is increased in the land.

"But put forth thine hand now, and touch all that he hath, and he will curse thee to thy face.

"And the Lord said unto Satan, Behold, all that he hath is in thy power; only upon himself put not forth thine hand. So Satan went forth from the presence of the Lord."

And a couple of verses from chapter 2, 6 and 7.

"And the Lord said unto Satan, Behold, he is in thine hand; but save his life.

"So went Satan forth from the presence of the Lord, and smote Job with sore boils from the sole of his foot unto his crown."

We know that Job became very discouraged and depressed because of all which happened to him. But, I wonder, if you or I were to face what Job went through, would we be able to keep ourselves from becoming discouraged and even depressed? Maybe if we were made of stone we could. I know from experience that often it has taken much less than what Job went through to make me feel discouraged and even depressed.

Now whose fault was it that Job became discouraged and depressed? Was it Job's own doing? God's Word tells us that Job was a very godly and upright person who hated evil. This does not mean that he was without sin. The Bible tells us all have sinned. But Job was a mature man of God, and by the grace of God, he lived a godly life. And the Bible tells us that he prayed and was concerned about the spiritual well-being of his children.

We can dare believe that many other people who lived during the time of Job, and who did not walk as close to God as Job did faced far less trial, far less stress, than Job did. We can't blame Job for what happened to him.

Now it is interesting to note as we read the book of Job, that Job felt that God was responsible for what was happening to him. But at the same time, he didn't blame God, but believed that God had a good reason for letting, or permitting, all which happened. In chapter 6, verse 4, we read, and Job is speaking, "For the arrows of the Almighty are within me, the poison whereof drinketh up my spirit: the terrors of God do set themselves in array against me." And there are other places in the Book of Job, where Job seems to think that God is accountable for what was happening to him.

But we also see from our text that

Satan was directly involved in what happened to Job.

There were enemies such as the Sabeans and the Chaldeans, which are mentioned in chapter one, who were involved and who killed and stole Job's livestock. Couldn't God have protected Job from such enemies? Oh we believe He could have.

And there was fire from heaven which could have been lightning. And there was wind which could have been a strong gale or a tornado, and which killed still more of Job's livestock, destroyed property and killed Job's children. In all of this most of Job's servants were killed. Only those who brought the sad news to Job were spared.

We usually think of God as the one in control of the weather. We do see in our text that God let Satan use the fire from heaven and wind to destroy Job's assets and kill his children.

When Jesus stilled the storm on the Sea of Galilee while in a boat with His disciples, the disciples marveled that the winds and waves were obedient to Jesus, the Son of God.

Was Job wrong when he felt that God was accountable for what happened to him?

But there is this difference between God and Satan: Satan loves to destroy because he has an evil heart, while God is a God of love and has plans to turn what may seem bad to us into something good for His beloved children.

"And we know that all things work together for good to them that love God, to them who are the called according to his purpose" (Rom. 8:28).

You see then that God has a purpose in all of this. However, to the non-Christian, if he doesn't repent but remains a non-Christian, all things will not turn out for good for him.

We may wonder about all of the natural disasters happening today, the hurricanes, earthquakes, floods, etc. Is this God's doing, or Satan's? When we realize the sinfulness of our nation and the world which allows the killing of unborn babies by the millions, the much lust and greed which is prevalent everywhere, and every other sin imaginable that mankind is guilty of, we might wonder that even worse things are not happening.

But how about the Christians? They suffer right along with the non-Christian as the result of an evil trend. We don't suffer only because we have sinned but we also suffer because we are in a sinful world.

Jesus had no sin and He suffered because He was in a sinful world. But God turned that into good. Jesus, by dying on the cross, took upon Himself the curse of sin.

God also wills to turn the suffering of the Christian into good. Do people turn to God and praise Him when they prosper because of His much goodness to them? No, so often when all goes well, people tend to forget God and their love for God turns into a love for the world and the things of the world.

Because of man's sinful nature it seems to take trial, suffering, stress and the like to cause people to remember God and turn to Him. It is sad, indeed, that it is this way. One might imagine that the more God does for the people the more they would appreciate Him and praise Him, but the very opposite seems to be the case so many times.

Now if God allowed, or willed that which happened to Job to happen to some liberals who scoff at God's Word, or if it happened to atheists or worldly, ungodly people, we wouldn't be surprised and might understand why it happened. But, instead, it happened to Job--a mature, righteous person.

Some would ask, "Why Job?" or, "Why me, when I have surrendered my life to Jesus and by God's grace am doing my best to live as God would will that I live?" There were some things that God wanted to teach and impress upon Job. This saying is often heard, "God is not finished with me yet."

When Job suddenly lost most of his property, family and later his health, it hit him like a sudden fierce storm and he became somewhat confused. Why would God allow such things to happen to Job who loved God and believed in righteousness? Job concluded that it would have been better if he had never been born. We read how Job felt about all that happened to him in the third chapter of Job.

But then as time went on, or as we read further on in the book of Job, Job said: "But He (God) knoweth the way that I take: when He hath tried me, I shall come forth as gold" (Job 23:10). This means that as a result of the losses and stressful situation which he faced he would become of even more value to God.

Job was already, very likely, the most godly person of his time. But God would mold him, temper him and make him a still better person. And this was God's purpose in leading Job through this most trying time in his life.

It was Satan who destroyed Job's livestock, killed his family, and caused his body to be infected with boils, because God permitted it, and because Satan loved to destroy. But God would have the final say and work all that Satan intended to be evil into good. Very likely Job was a strong influence for godliness in the community and country in which he lived.

But God wanted to prepare Job for still greater use, and what Satan tore down, God intended to build up again to be better than it had been before.

At first Job couldn't understand God's ways. Sometimes it is also difficult for us to understand God's ways, but then if we remain faithful and with God's help or grace "just hang in there," sooner or later we will realize that God's intent is always to do good to those who trust Him and will to obey Him.

Now God has given us His Word, the Bible, and herein is everything that God wants to teach us. And as we dig into this book we soon discover that there is enough learning here to last us for a lifetime and then some. No one has ever been able to exhaust all that can be learned from this book, the Bible, in a lifetime.

But we also tend to forget. It is so easy to just have God's truth in our heads and not in our hearts. It is so easy to know God's Word but not really take it seriously.

But God has His ways of impressing His truth upon us. And He does this differently with different people. He had a way of impressing His truth upon Jeremiah and in that which He wanted Jeremiah to seriously take to heart.

Jeremiah had been called by God to be a prophet but it was not an easy work that God had called Jeremiah to do. In fact it was a very discouraging work. Jeremiah has been referred to as the weeping prophet for this very reason. He had a message from God which he was to preach to the people. But the people didn't take to heart what Jeremiah said to them.

One day God told Jeremiah to wear

his girdle and to make a long trip across the desert, which would be very difficult travel, to the Euphrates River. If you look on the map you will see that the Euphrates River is a long distance east of Palestine. It must have taken Jeremiah several days of hard travel to make this trip.

And when Jeremiah finally got to the Euphrates River he was told to take off his girdle (or sash, as we would call it) and hide it in the rocks near the river. Jeremiah did as he was told and made the long trip back across the desert to his home in Palestine.

After many days God told Jeremiah to now go to the Euphrates River and dig up his girdle from among the rocks where he had buried it, which Jeremiah did without question. But when he dug up the girdle what do you think Jeremiah found? Nothing unusual, but only that which you might expect. The girdle was marred and became quite useless.

And then God said to Jeremiah, "If my people don't repent of their sinful, wicked ways, the same thing will happen to them as what happened to this girdle. They will decay as a people. And, Jeremiah, I want you to tell them this."

The purpose of a girdle (or sash) is not that it should be buried in the rocks but to wear close to the body. It will only be ruined by the dampness of the earth. Even as a sash is worn close to the body, so people, those whom God created, must stay close to God. But if they wander away from Him and love the world and the things of the world more than they love God, they, like the girdle, will only decay and be destroyed. So it would be with God's people if they didn't repent of their sin and stay close to God.

Well, what happened? Jeremiah delivered

God's message to the people, but they didn't heed it, and God permitted an enemy to capture them and to take them as prisoners far from their homeland where they became enslaved.

Then Jeremiah was persecuted by the people and became unpopular as the result of preaching what God told him to preach.

But why did God have Jeremiah make this long trip through a hot desert just to see a girdle? It was an object lesson which God willed to impress upon Jeremiah. If God had told Jeremiah to bury his girdle in the back yard the result would have been the same, and Jeremiah wouldn't have had to undergo all that hard, long travel.

But God wanted Jeremiah not only to realize what his calling was, but God also wanted to impress it upon Jeremiah so he wouldn't forget and perhaps be tempted to preach a more popular message to the people.

Now does God ever act this way in our day? Yes, I believe He does. I believe He has dealt with me in a similar way. In 1964, 30 years ago, I went through a time of very deep depression. It was so severe that I spent most of a year in a hospital. And I didn't know why God allowed this to happen to me. For a long time I couldn't figure out what made me so depressed. But after a number of months God did heal me, and He worked it all out for good. I feel in my own heart that I learned much from that period of depression. I have often said that it was like a schooling to me.

Not only did God heal me, but He impressed some truths upon me--as he had to Jeremiah--in order that I wouldn't soon forget them. And these truths were not so much new truths which I had never heard before, but they took on a new importance after having suffered depression.

However, I am still learning. I am

sure God is not through with me, although I am an old man now. God has something to teach us as long as we remain on earth.

My point is that God did work out my time with depression for good. I can truly thank Him for it now.

I wonder if Jeremiah ever regretted having to make those long, hot, wearisome journeys through the desert. I doubt it. God was real to Jeremiah and although his work was discouraging here on earth, he never hesitated in doing what God expected of him, and his reward awaits him in heaven.

But now let me say something about discouragement and even depression.

I can remember as a boy on the farm that my brother and I would sometimes hire out to one of our neighbors for a day or several days to plow corn, make hay, shock grain, or whatever our neighbor needed.

We worked long hours. We would start at seven in the morning or a little before and we would work until six or a little later at night. Our wage was $1.00 a day. And how very happy and proud we were to be able to come home at night with a dollar in our pockets which we could show to our parents.

But we also came home very weary and tired. We had spent the energy we woke up with that morning in working for our neighbor. We fully gave of our strength and ability during the day. And the same was expected of us. But before we left at the end of the day we were given a big meal.

Or we can think of the soldier on the battle field. At times he has to put in long hours of fighting the enemy under very trying conditions. He too gets tired and hungry. Sometimes he gets wounded, hurt and even killed. And it is expected of him to give of himself in this way.

But then as he gets hungry, the army

feeds him. And when he gets tired at night the army provides a place for him to sleep or rest as best they can under the conditions. And if he gets hurt or wounded they provide first aid stations and hospitals.

Now the point I want to make is this. When my brother and I came home from working all day my father and mother never said to us, "Oh, but you shouldn't have allowed yourselves to become tired."

When the soldier on the battlefield gets tired, weary, discouraged or wounded, no one that I saw (and I was in the army during the second world war for almost three years) ever said, "Oh but you shouldn't have allowed yourself to become tired, discouraged or wounded," as if it were the soldier's fault that this happened to him. No, although the army expected the soldier to give of himself in battle, when he became hungry, tired, discouraged or wounded they were there to help and sustain him in his need.

Now what is my point? Just this: There are those who would say to the Christian warrior, "You should never allow yourself to become tired, weary, discouraged, or depressed as the result of facing and fighting the Christian warfare and if you really have faith in Jesus this would never happen to you. As a Christian you should be able to ride above these things because if you have enough faith Jesus will not allow such weariness and discouragement to overtake you. He will keep you joyous and happy at all times. You need not worry or be anxious or concerned about anything."

Now it is true that there are things which we can do to ward off feelings of weariness, discouragement and depression to some extent. Just like the worker can do certain things to prevent himself from getting too exhausted or overly tired early in the day. For example he can take short rest periods, take a noon break and take time to eat. He needs to be careful so as not to tear into his work too fast or too hard so as not to get all worn out before the day comes to an end or before the work is finished.

And the same is true of the soldier on the battlefield. He is trained to take certain precautions

The same is true of the Christian soldier. He can pray. He can read and study his Bible. He can take encouragement from Christian friends, etc.

But, nevertheless, the Christian warfare is not an easy warfare--and it is all around us every day on all sides. And no matter how careful a soldier may be, there comes a time when a rest is needed. We are all human. And sometimes discouragement and depression overtake us because of no fault of our own. And this is why Jesus said in Matthew 11:28: "Come unto me, all ye that labour and are heavy laden, and I will give you rest".

And God knows our limitations. Psalm 103:14, says: For He knoweth our frame; He remembereth that we are dust".

Although God is almighty and powerful He knows that we have our limitations. He doesn't expect the impossible of us. He doesn't expect us to endure under pressure and stress for long periods of time and remain unmoved. He will allow us to become tired and weary at times, almost to the breaking point. At least it may seem so to us.

But God has a purpose in this also. We become strengthened through it. When iron is put in the fire, it gets very soft and bendable when red hot with little or no strength to hold anything up. But then as it cools again it becomes stronger than ever. It becomes steel.

In Psalm 37:23, 24, we have these words: "The steps of a good man are ordered by the Lord: and he delighteth in his way. Though he fall, he shall not be utterly cast down: for the Lord upholdeth him with his hand." So it was with Job. Job was severely tested, and Job credited God for so testing him.

Elijah, too, a mature man of God, at one time became very discouraged. (I Kings 19:4). It seemed to him that he was the only one left who still had faith in the Lord God. It seemed that all his efforts in serving the Lord, and winning souls for Him, had been effort done in vain. How would you have felt if it seemed to you that you were the only one left in the whole wide world that remained faithful to God?

But then when God spoke to Elijah on Mount Horeb he didn't appear in the wind or the earthquake (which would have been symbolic of God's wrath) but He spoke in an encouraging way in a still, small, gentle voice. This should tell us that God was not displeased with Elijah.

And then God assured Elijah that there were still 7,000 people who had not bowed down to Baal. No doubt God had used Elijah in winning many of these 7,000 unto Himself. Elijah was now encouraged. God gave Elijah new hope.

Some believe that God was critical of Elijah at this time for having become discouraged but I believe that God was giving new hope to Elijah and not criticizing him. I don't believe that God is critical of those who become discouraged, disheartened or depressed as the result of fighting the Christian warfare. He gives new hope to such warriors.

In Matthew 11:28 we have Jesus famous words: "Come unto me, all ye that labour and are heavy laden, and I will give you rest." It is the one who has worked who is invited to come for rest. And it is because the labourer went out into the field (God's harvest field of souls) that he has need of rest. In these words of Jesus we see no words of rebuke for the labourer.

I am afraid that Christians too often tend to avoid the harvest field where there is sweat and dirt for fear of losing the joy and peaceful existence they so enjoy by being a Christian. (I also speak to myself as I say this.) We want to fight the Christian warfare in our own homes or in church among other Christians, where we can feel secure and don't need to get our hands dirty. This is not the kind of example Jesus gave us. He came into this world and readily mixed with the people without being taken in by the world so that He could win some unto Himself. And it is not the example that Jesus' disciples left with us. We believe (with the exception of one) they gave their lives in an effort to spread the Gospel.

But we don't face the Christian warfare alone. Jesus has said, "Lo, I am with you always." We can count on Jesus to go with us as we go out into the world to win souls for Jesus. May God help us!

VIII. APPENDIX

38. Some Stresses That May Contribute To Depression

1. Taking on too much work or responsibility. The mind is not able to rest when the body rests, but continues to think about the work not finished. Such a person, like Martha (Luke 10:38-42), does not take enough time to nourish the soul with the Word of God.

2. Working for long periods of time in stressful situations. It is better for your mental health to have work you enjoy even though the pay is less.

3. Continued disappointment or unrealized ambitions, especially after working hard to attain them.

4. Pressure from the world to conform to its ways and beliefs. The world may brand you as an oddball for not consenting to its ways. Throughout history Christians have been known to undergo all types of persecution by the world. Persecution can be wearing on one's mental health, but be of good cheer, for it is far better to bring glory to Jesus' name, even at a strain to mental health, than to conform to the ways of the world. Neither will Jesus forsake you. To find a Christian fellowship or join a good Bible study group will help to relieve the pressure or stress in a situation such as this.

5. Going against your convictions, letting yourself be talked into doing something which goes against your conscience or which you have no freedom to do. Worldly friends often tempt the Christian in this way.

6. Fear of having done something foolish, or fear of having wronged someone. It is helpful to confess such fears to a

trustworthy Christian friend or pastor, and have him or her help you to bring them to God in prayer, who readily forgives, if there is any true guilt. After confessing such things to God you have every right to put such things out of your mind as if you had never done anything wrong.

7. Guilt from losing your temper, especially to a friend or close relative. Note: One of the symptoms of clinical depression is a short temper--shorter than usual. The depressed person is not his normal self. The stress he is under causes him to be impatient.

8. Financial stress. The wise Christian is careful not to overbuy on credit, and have no money with which to meet emergencies. God has promised that if we "seek" first the kingdom of God and His righteousness, all our needs will be provided (Matt. 6:33). However, God's promise does not give liberty to overspend.

9. Disagreement with someone who can affect your life such as an employer, neighbor or close relative. We need to seek God's wisdom, patience and love in dealing with people who affect our life but whom we find difficult to get along with.

10. Accepting false teaching, or false doctrine. God may check you with acute depression, as He did me, if you go too far to the left or right from sound Biblical doctrine.

11. Fear of the future or some illness. Since God is our refuge, we need not fear. Most of our fears are never realized, and if they are, God gives sustaining grace. However, we need to face our fears, ever seeking God's wisdom in knowing how to confront them. Find out, as best you can, how realistic your fears are, ever seeking the comforts and promises of God's Word.

The wrong thing to do is to try to forget them by pushing them into your subconscious mind.

    12. A health problem of your own or that of a dear friend or relative.

    13. Carrying the guilt of unforgiven sin.

39. Symptoms of Acute or Clinical Depression

1. Feelings of depression and uncertainty.
2. Worry and anxiety, even when there is not sufficient cause for them.
3. Difficulty in doing little things which you once did quite naturally. Even such a simple thing as taking a bath can become a mountainous task causing great concern before it is done.
4. No feeling of accomplishment even after a task is finished.
5. Inability to complete a task to your own satisfaction.
6. Loss of memory.
7. Inability to concentrate, plan or organize activity.
8. A continuous feeling of having forgotten something.
9. A feeling that God has deserted you.
10. Feelings of great guilt.
11. Fear that you are being unfair or discourteous to friends and loved ones, or not expressing enough appreciation to them.
12. Mental blocks. You start to say something and forget what you were going to say.
13. Inability to follow conversation, to read and concentrate on what you are reading. You may find it hard and even impossible to read the Bible.
14. A short temper--shorter than usual.
15. Not being able to pray or concentrate on prayer.
16. Having a sense of need to express inner feelings and frustrations to someone, but being unable to find the words to express or describe those feelings, even to a doctor.
17. Great feelings of inadequacy in doing the work and responsibility which

is expected of you.

18. Inability to find anything enjoyable in life. Everything becomes tedious.

19. Loss of appetite.

20. Difficulty in sleeping, and a constant tired feeling--even after waking.

21. Extreme feelings of loneliness, boredom, listlessness, and restlessness.

22. A loss of meaning to life.

23. A desire to die.

Note: It is normal to have some of these symptoms at times. However, if they become accelerated in your life, you do best if you seek help from a Christian doctor, pastor or friend.

40. How to Maintain or Regain Your Mental Health

Following are a few practical suggestions for the Christian to maintain his mental health:

1. Continue to like yourself, even when depressed. It is no more disgraceful for a Christian to be depressed than it is for a soldier to be wounded in battle.

2. Be assured that God loves you, and that He has not forgotten you.

3. Be patient, better days are coming. You will again be all you once were and more. You will be enriched for having gone through the experience of depression. You will again be able to enjoy all the things you once did and much, much more. God has promised to work all things out for good for the Christian (Rom. 8:28).

4. Do not blame yourself for getting depressed. Chances are that it is not your fault. We live in a world and in an age where there are many stressful situations which are depressing to the Christian.

5. Do not panic because of such symptoms as temporary loss of concentration, memory blocks, inability to express yourself clearly, and others. Your former abilities will all be restored to you in due time.

6. Try, as best you can, to seek enjoyment wherever you can, although it is difficult when depressed. Many former enjoyments no longer appeal, but try, nevertheless. Let your friends know of the things you do enjoy or things you might enjoy, so that they can help you find enjoyment and suggest things that you might enjoy. Enjoyment helps to bring release from depression.

7. As previously mentioned, avoid being idle. Make an effort to become involved in some project, but take ample time to

relax and rest when you feel the need.

8. Get involved in some physical activity, work or play that does not take a lot of concentration. Avoid that which would cause nervous strain. A tired body, due to work or wholesome play, will help a worried and stress-ridden mind to relax and sleep better at night.

9. Do not stay at one thing so long that it becomes tiresome.

10. Do not think that what you are doing is not worthwhile if it isn't earning you money. If you enjoy doing it, if it helps you to become involved, it is worthwhile and will help to bring healing. If you enjoy it, and it is not a sin--do it.

11. As far as possible, avoid doing things which depress you.

12. It may be good for you, if possible, to go on a vacation or to get away from familiar surroundings for a while. However if this does not appeal, it may not be the right thing to do. If you should have a strong desire to get away for a while but can't see how that is possible, ask God to help you find a way.

13. As far as possible, without sinning, do that which is natural and appealing. I like to take long walks and enjoy the beauty of nature.

14. If depressed, sleep when you can sleep. You need your rest. However, avoid tossing on your bed if sleep does not come. It is best to get up for a while and then try to get some sleep a little later.

15. Find what comfort and strength you can in reading your Bible and in praying. But if you find this to be difficult because of depression (as it was with me), do not let it worry you. God understands. Feed your soul on whatever Bible knowledge you have stored in your memory until that time

when you can better concentrate on what you read. If you can't pray long prayers, pray short sentence prayers.

16. Share your faith, give your testimony, and share Bible truths with others whenever you have the opportunity or when you find someone who will listen. Avoid religious arguments. You may feel that you have little to share or that no one would be very interested in hearing from a depressed person. But it is often in our weakness that God can best use us. This was, also, Paul's experience (II Cor. 12:10). It is a joy and a source of healing to share that which is spiritual with someone else.

17. Seek fellowship, especially Christian fellowship. It is always good to talk with someone, especially if that someone shows love and concern for you and your problems.

18. As far as possible, avoid those who depress you. Beware of unsound advice and poor counseling. There are always those who think they have the answer when they don't. If you are not sure about something, don't let it confuse you and don't accept it as truth until you are sure that it is the truth or good advice. It is always good to check it out with a Christian friend whom you can trust.

19. Make the most of what God has made available to you, such as sunshine, flowers, birds, seasons of the year, family and friends.

20. Dare to believe those who encourage you in some way. Take compliments to heart and let them inspire you to continue to do good.

21. Never take on any more work or responsibility than what you can manage without being under pressure. Learn to say "no" even to friends when it becomes

necessary.
    22. Do not let Satan or anyone else make you feel guilty for things you didn't do, couldn't help, or for deeds which are not sinful.

41. Some Suggestions For Helping A Depressed Loved One

1. Assure him (or her) of God's love and that He has not deserted him.
2. Be honest and truthful in all of your association with him.
3. Give all the encouragement that you can. Remind him of his strong points and of how he has been a help and blessing to you and to others. Reassure him that he will again be able to function as he once did. Avoid criticism or making him feel guilty. Encourage but do not flatter.
4. In his presence pray for him. Assure him that you will continue to pray for him.
5. Point out encouraging signs of returning health as they occur.
6. Help him to work out solutions to his immediate worries and problems. See that he gets the help he needs to do the work that is expected of him. Release him from as many worries and responsibilities as you can.
7. Continue to assure him of your love and concern.
8. Allow for a short temper, impatience, and any other unlikeable traits due to his illness.
9. Be willing to listen to what is on his heart. If he is very depressed suggest that he seek help. Assure him that it is no disgrace to do so. You may be able to assist him in finding the needed help.
10. Quote Bible verses which speak of Jesus' love for sinners. Expound on these truths, putting the truth in your own words; but avoid throwing too much Bible at him--more than what he can comprehend at that time. Be very careful that you do not become offensive. Do not use the

Bible (at this time) to convict of sin, but to comfort and encourage.

11. If you are not a member of the family, be careful not to overstay your time so as to make your visit wearisome. Many short visits are better than a few long ones.

12. Help him to think through and make everyday decisions. It is difficult for the acutely depressed to make decisions. Yet beware that you do not make all decisions for him, making him feel useless or unimportant.

13. Help him to like himself. Reassure him that he is likeable and has much to offer in the way of fellowship and help.

14. Show him the same love and respect as always. Do nothing that would make him feel inferior because of his depression.

15. As he regains health, help him to gradually take on the responsibility and duties he once had.

16. The depressed person desires that someone might understand his feelings and help him to express them. He often finds it difficult and even impossible to do so. If you can do this or find someone who can, you will be a big help to him. Someone who has had a similar experience of suffering, or depression, can do this best (II Cor. 1:4).

17. Encourage him to be patient, and to wait on God.

ABOUT THE AUTHOR

Gerald Frederick Mundfrom, son of Edward and Amanda Mundfrom, was born August 9, 1917, on a farm near Tripoli, Iowa. He was baptized and confirmed in the Lutheran faith. He spent almost three years in the Army during World War II, during which time he had his first experience with acute depression. He is a graduate of Luther College, Decorah, Iowa, and Luther Theological Seminary, St. Paul, Minnesota, and was ordained in September of 1950. He married Margaret Lindquist and is the father of six children. He has served as a parish pastor in Minnesota and North and South Dakota.

Pastor Mundfrom has felt God's hand upon him from early childhood and believes it was God's will that he serve Him in a full-time way and as His spirit would lead.

In 1964, while serving as pastor in rural Veblen, South Dakota, he again suffered an acute siege of depression and spent months in a mental hospital. He tells of this experience and how God led and guided him through it in his book entitled, "Purged," published in 1979. It was reprinted under a new title, "My Experience with Clinical Depression," in 1990.

Since 1970 Pastor Mundfrom has been engaged in a traveling, speaking, and writing ministry. He is a member of the clergy of the Association of Free Lutheran Congregations and director of Mercy and Truth Publishers which publishes his writings. Besides his two books on depression he is the author of "Baptism, A Covenant," "The Threat of False Doctrine," and numerous shorter writings and sermons.